Mastering Grant Writing:

A Nonprofit's Guide to Effective Proposal Development and Submission

By

QUEEN ISRAEL

Disclaimer

First and foremost, the information provided in this book is intended to be educational and informative, but it is not intended to be a substitute for legal or financial advice. While the authors have done their best to provide accurate and up-to-date information, laws and regulations regarding grants and funding can vary depending on the country, state, or region, and it is important to consult with professionals in the field to ensure compliance with all applicable laws and regulations.

Additionally, this book does not guarantee success in obtaining grant funding. While the authors have provided guidance and best practices based on their experiences and research, the grant writing process can be highly competitive, and there are many factors that can impact the success of a grant proposal.

It is also important to note that the examples and case studies provided in this book are meant to be illustrative and are not necessarily applicable to every situation. Every nonprofit and grant proposal is unique, and it is important to tailor strategies and approaches to fit specific needs and goals.

This book is not an exhaustive guide to grant writing and management. There are many resources available to nonprofits seeking to improve their grant writing skills, and it is important to continue learning and seeking out new information and best practices.

In summary, while this book provides valuable insights and guidance for nonprofits seeking to improve their grant writing and management skills, it is important to approach the information with a critical and discerning eye, and to seek out professional advice when necessary. By being aware of the limitations and disclaimers of the information provided, nonprofits can use this resource as a tool to help them make a lasting impact through effective grant writing and management.

Preface

Welcome to the world of grant writing, a realm of nonprofit work that holds tremendous potential for impact and innovation. Whether you are a seasoned grant writer or new to the field, this book is designed to provide you with the tools and resources necessary to craft winning grant proposals that will help you secure the funding you need to create lasting change.

Through years of experience in the nonprofit sector, I have come to appreciate the importance of grant writing as a powerful tool for building a sustainable, impactful organization.

Effective grant writing can help you develop strong relationships with funders, engage in productive collaborations with partners and stakeholders, and build a culture of grant readiness that will serve your organization for years to come.

In this book, you will learn how to navigate the grant writing process from start to finish, beginning with the crucial task of identifying potential funders and crafting a compelling proposal. We will explore the key components of a successful grant proposal, from the executive summary to the budget narrative, and provide practical tips and strategies for each step of the process.

In addition to mastering the art of grant writing, this book will also help you develop the skills and expertise necessary to effectively manage the grant funds you receive, communicate with funders and stakeholders, and create accurate and timely reports.

Through case studies and real-world examples, you will gain valuable insights into how top-performing nonprofits have overcome common grant writing challenges, such as limited staff capacity and lack of experience, and achieved success through effective collaboration with partners and funders.

At the heart of this book is the belief that successful grant writing is not just about securing funding, but also about building relationships and making a lasting impact on the world. I hope that the tools, strategies, and stories contained within these pages will inspire you to think big and pursue your organization's goals with passion and purpose.

So, let's get started on the journey to mastering grant writing for lasting impact!

Dedication

To all the hardworking staff and volunteers at nonprofits around the world, who work tirelessly every day to make a positive impact in their communities. Your dedication and passion inspire us all to strive for a better world. This book is dedicated to you.

Acknowledgements

Firstly, I would like to express my deepest gratitude to my son, Elvis, who has been a constant source of inspiration and support throughout this project. Your unwavering belief in my abilities and your encouragement to pursue my passions have been invaluable to me. Your boundless energy, creativity, and curiosity have reminded me to approach this book with the same sense of wonder and enthusiasm that you bring to your own pursuits. I am truly blessed to have you as my son, and I thank you for being a constant source of joy and motivation in my life.

Secondly, I would like to acknowledge the unwavering support of my husband, Samuel. Your love, encouragement, and patience have been essential to the completion of this project. Your willingness to listen to my ideas, provide feedback, and offer words of encouragement when I was feeling discouraged, have made this journey less daunting. Your selflessness and unwavering belief in my abilities have allowed me to pursue my passions with confidence and determination. Thank you for being my rock and for always believing in me.

In addition to my son and husband, I would also like to thank the numerous colleagues, friends, and mentors who have supported me throughout this project. Their feedback, insights, and encouragement have been invaluable in shaping the content of this book.

Lastly, I would like to thank my readers for their interest in this book. I hope that it provides you with the guidance, insights, and inspiration that you need to succeed in your own grant writing endeavors.

Contents

Chapter 1 10

Introduction to Grant Writing.................................10

Chapter 2..24

Identifying Potential Funding Sources 24

Chapter 3 40

Preparing to write a Grant.......................................40

Chapter 4 55

Writing the Grant Proposal......................................55

Chapter 5 67

Creating Effective Supporting Materials...................67

Chapter 6: 79

Submitting the Grant Proposal 79

Chapter 7 89

Post submission, what happens next? 89

Chapter 8 99

Stewarding the grant...99

Chapter 9 107

Common Grant writing challenges and solutions 107

Chapter 10: 119

Best Practices for Successful Grant Writing............................119

Chapter 11: 130

Conclusion: Mastering Grant Writing for Lasting Impact 130

Chapter 1
Introduction to Grant Writing

Nonprofits play a crucial role in our communities. They work to solve important social and environmental issues that impact our daily lives. These organizations often rely on grants as a major source of funding to carry out their missions. Grants are offered by a variety of organizations, including government agencies, private foundations, corporations, and individual donors.

While there are many different types of grants available, the process for applying for them is generally similar. The first step in the grant writing process is to identify potential funding sources. This involves researching and evaluating available grants to find the ones that best align with your organization's mission and goals.

Once you've identified potential funders, the next step is to prepare to write your grant proposal. This involves organizing your team and resources, developing a project plan and budget, and defining your project goals and objectives. Writing the proposal itself is a major part of the grant writing process, and it's important to craft a compelling narrative that meets the funder's expectations and guidelines.

One common mistake that many nonprofits make when writing grant proposals is failing to understand the funder's priorities and requirements. Each funder is unique, and it's important to tailor your proposal to their specific needs and interests. Failure to do so can lead to a rejected proposal, even if the project itself is strong.

Another common mistake is submitting a proposal that is poorly organized or difficult to read. Funders often receive many proposals, and it's important to make yours stand out by presenting your information in a clear and concise manner.

To avoid these mistakes, it's important to take the time to thoroughly research potential funders and understand their expectations. It's also important to organize your proposal in a way that is easy to read and understand, with a clear narrative that demonstrates how your project will achieve the funder's goals and priorities.

In this book, you are provided with the tools and knowledge you need to master the grant writing process and write successful proposals that effectively communicate your organization's mission and goals. I cover everything from identifying potential funding sources to submitting your proposal and managing your grant funds.

I also provided practical examples and case studies throughout the book to help you understand how real-world nonprofits have successfully navigated the grant writing process.

By the end of this book, you'll have the skills and confidence you need to develop and submit effective grant proposals that help your organization make a meaningful impact on your community.

The importance of Grants for Nonprofits

Nonprofits are critical to our society, working to address social, environmental, and cultural issues that impact our daily lives. However, the work of nonprofits often requires significant resources, and funding can be a major challenge. This is where grants come in - they provide an essential source of funding for nonprofits to carry out their missions and make a positive impact on the world.

Grants are offered by a variety of organizations, including government agencies, private foundations, corporations, and individual donors. These organizations often have a specific mission or focus area, and they provide grants to nonprofits that align with their goals and priorities.

The importance of grants for nonprofits cannot be overstated. They provide a significant source of funding that can help organizations achieve their missions and make a meaningful impact on their communities. Grants can support a wide range of activities, including program development, research, capacity building, and infrastructure development.

In addition to providing financial support, grants can also help to increase the visibility and credibility of a nonprofit. By receiving a grant from a reputable organization, a nonprofit can demonstrate its effectiveness and impact to potential donors and stakeholders. This can lead to increased funding and support in the future.

Grants can also help to foster innovation and creativity within nonprofits. By providing funding for new programs or initiatives, grants can allow nonprofits to try out new ideas and approaches without the fear of financial risk. This can lead to the development of new solutions to social and environmental challenges, and can ultimately lead to more effective and efficient services for the community.

However, it's important to note that the grant application process can be competitive and challenging. There are often many nonprofits vying for the same funding opportunities, and the process of identifying potential funders and preparing a strong proposal can be time-consuming and resource-intensive.

To increase the likelihood of receiving a grant, it's important for nonprofits to develop a strong understanding of the funding landscape and to carefully target their proposals to specific funders. This requires significant research and preparation, as well as a deep understanding of the funder's goals and priorities.

Once a grant is awarded, it's important for nonprofits to effectively manage the funds and to meet the requirements set out by the funder. This involves careful planning, budgeting, and reporting to ensure that the grant funds are used effectively and efficiently.

In conclusion, grants are essential source of funding for nonprofits to carry out their missions and make a positive impact on the world. They provide financial support, increase visibility and credibility, and foster innovation and creativity. While the grant application process can be competitive and challenging, with the right preparation and approach, nonprofits can increase their chances of success and effectively manage their grant funds to make a meaningful difference in their communities.

The Grant Writing Process

Grant writing can be a daunting process for nonprofits, requiring significant research, planning, and attention to detail. However, with the right approach and tools, it can also be a highly rewarding process that can provide essential funding for important programs and initiatives.

In this chapter, we'll explore the grant writing process in detail, outlining the key steps that nonprofits should take to prepare a strong and effective grant proposal.

Step 1: Identify Funding Opportunities

The first step in the grant writing process is to identify potential funding opportunities that align with the nonprofit's mission and programs. This involves researching various foundations, corporations, government agencies, and other potential funders, and identifying those that have a mission or focus area that matches the nonprofit's needs.

It's important to carefully review the guidelines and requirements for each potential funder, and to ensure that the nonprofit's programs and initiatives are a good fit. This may involve reaching out to the funder to ask questions or gather additional information about their funding priorities and requirements.

Step 2: Develop a Proposal

Once potential funders have been identified, the next step is to develop a strong and effective proposal. This involves outlining the nonprofit's programs and initiatives, as well as its goals and objectives. The proposal should clearly and compellingly demonstrate how the nonprofit's work aligns with the funder's priorities, and how the proposed program or initiative will make a meaningful impact on the community.

The proposal should also include a detailed budget that outlines the costs associated with the proposed program or initiative, as well as any other sources of funding or in-kind support that will be used to cover these costs.

Step 3: Write the Grant Application

With the proposal in hand, it's time to write the grant application itself. This typically involves filling out an online or paper application form, as well as providing any additional documentation or information required by the funder.

It's important to carefully review the application requirements and guidelines, and to ensure that all questions are answered fully and accurately. Nonprofits should also pay close attention to the formatting and structure of the application, and ensure that it is clear, concise, and well-organized.

Step 4: Submit the Application

Once the grant application has been completed, it's time to submit it to the funder. This may involve mailing a hard copy of the application, or submitting it online through the funder's website or grant management system.

It's important to carefully review the submission requirements and deadlines, and to ensure that the application is submitted on time and in the correct format.

Nonprofits should also keep a copy of the application and any supporting documentation for their records.

Step 5: Follow Up and Reporting

After the grant application has been submitted, the nonprofit should follow up with the funder to ensure that it has been received and to inquire about the timeline for the review process. If the grant is awarded, the nonprofit should carefully manage the funds and ensure that all reporting requirements are met in a timely and accurate manner.

If the grant is not awarded, it's important to review the feedback provided by the funder and to use this information to improve future grant proposals. Nonprofits should also continue to seek out new funding opportunities and work to build relationships with potential funders.

Final Thoughts: The grant writing process can be a challenging but rewarding endeavor for nonprofits. By carefully identifying potential funders, developing strong proposals, and submitting well-crafted grant applications, nonprofits can secure essential funding to support their programs and initiatives. It's also important to follow up and manage the grant funds effectively, and to use the feedback from the process to continually improve grant proposals and increase the likelihood of future success.

Common Mistakes to Avoid

Grant writing is a crucial process for nonprofits seeking funding to support their programs and initiatives. While it can be a challenging and time-consuming process, the potential rewards can be substantial. However, there are several common mistakes that nonprofits can make in the grant writing process that can significantly reduce their chances of success. In this chapter, we'll explore some of the most common mistakes to avoid in grant writing, and provide guidance on how to steer clear of these pitfalls.

Mistake 1: Failing to Research Potential Funders

One of the most critical steps in the grant writing process is identifying potential funders that align with the nonprofit's mission and programs. However, many nonprofits make the mistake of not conducting thorough research to identify the best potential funders. This can lead to wasted time and effort on proposals that are unlikely to be successful.

To avoid this mistake, nonprofits should conduct in-depth research to identify potential funders that have a mission or focus area that aligns with their programs and initiatives. This involves reviewing the guidelines and requirements for each potential funder and ensuring that the nonprofit's programs and initiatives are a good fit. It may also involve reaching out to the funder to ask questions or gather additional information about their funding priorities and requirements.

Mistake 2: Failing to Customize the Proposal

Another common mistake in grant writing is failing to customize the proposal to fit the requirements and priorities of the potential funder. Many nonprofits make the mistake of using a generic proposal template for all potential funders, which can lead to proposals that are not well-matched to the funder's needs and priorities.

To avoid this mistake, nonprofits should carefully review the guidelines and requirements for each potential funder, and customize the proposal to fit their specific needs and priorities. This may involve tailoring the language and format of the proposal, as well as emphasizing certain aspects of the nonprofit's work that are particularly relevant to the funder's priorities.

Mistake 3: Failing to Clearly Articulate the Need and Impact

A common mistake in grant writing is failing to clearly articulate the need for the proposed program or initiative, as well as the potential impact it will have on the community. Many nonprofits make the mistake of providing vague or general statements about the need for the program, which can make it difficult for the funder to understand the importance and relevance of the proposed work.

To avoid this mistake, nonprofits should clearly and compellingly articulate the need for the proposed program or initiative, and demonstrate how it will make a meaningful impact on the community. This may involve using data and research to support the need for the program, as well as providing specific examples of the potential impact it will have.

Mistake 4: Failing to Follow the Guidelines and Requirements

One of the most common mistakes in grant writing is failing to follow the guidelines and requirements for the grant application. Many nonprofits make the mistake of submitting incomplete or incorrect applications, which can lead to immediate disqualification from the funding process.

To avoid this mistake, nonprofits should carefully review the guidelines and requirements for the grant application and ensure that all questions are answered fully and accurately. They should also pay close attention to the formatting and structure of the application, and ensure that it is clear, concise, and well-organized.

Mistake 5: Failing to Provide a Detailed Budget

Another common mistake in grant writing is failing to provide a detailed budget that outlines the costs associated with the proposed program or initiative. Many nonprofits make the mistake of providing vague or incomplete budget information, which can make it difficult for the funder to understand the full scope of the proposed work and how the funds will be used.

To avoid this mistake, nonprofits should provide a detailed budget that outlines all of the costs associated with the proposed program or initiative, including personnel, supplies, equipment, and any other expenses. The budget should be clear and transparent, and should demonstrate how the requested funds will be used to achieve the nonprofit's goals.

Mistake 6: Failing to Provide Clear and Measurable Objectives

Another common mistake in grant writing is failing to provide clear and measurable objectives for the proposed program or initiative. Many nonprofits make the mistake of providing vague or overly general objectives, which can make it difficult for the funder to understand the impact and effectiveness of the proposed work.

To avoid this mistake, nonprofits should provide clear and measurable objectives that are tied to specific outcomes and metrics. This may involve setting specific goals for the program, such as the number of people who will be served, the percentage of participants who will achieve certain outcomes, or the specific impact that will be achieved in the community. These objectives should be tied to specific metrics that can be tracked and evaluated over time.

Mistake 7: Failing to Demonstrate the Organization's Capacity to Implement the Program

A final common mistake in grant writing is failing to demonstrate the organization's capacity to effectively implement the proposed program or initiative. Many nonprofits make the mistake of providing vague or insufficient information about their organizational capacity, which can raise concerns for the funder about the nonprofit's ability to successfully implement the proposed work.

To avoid this mistake, nonprofits should provide clear and compelling information about their organizational capacity, including their experience and expertise in the program area, their staffing and resources, and their partnerships and collaborations. They should also demonstrate how they will monitor and evaluate the program to ensure that it is effective and achieves the desired outcomes.

Grant writing can be a challenging process for nonprofits, but avoiding common mistakes can significantly increase the chances of success. Nonprofits should conduct thorough research to identify potential funders, customize their proposals to fit the requirements and priorities of the funder, and clearly articulate the need and impact of the proposed program. They should also follow the guidelines and requirements for the grant application, provide a detailed budget, set clear and measurable objectives, and demonstrate their organizational capacity to implement the program. By avoiding these common mistakes, nonprofits can increase their chances of securing the funding they need to support their important work in the community.

CASE STUDY

Let me introduce you to a hypothetical nonprofit organization called "Community Builders". Community Builders is a nonprofit organization that is dedicated to building stronger and more vibrant communities across the United States. *The mission of Community Builders is to empower individuals and organizations to work together to address the most pressing issues facing their communities, including poverty, inequality, and lack of access to essential services.*

Community Builders was founded by a group of passionate and dedicated individuals who saw a need for a new approach to community development. They recognized that traditional approaches to community development often failed to engage residents and address the root causes of social and economic inequality. Community Builders was founded on the belief that effective community development requires a collaborative, grassroots approach that empowers residents and builds local capacity.

The goal of Community Builders is to create sustainable, community-led solutions to the most pressing issues facing communities across the United States. To achieve this goal, Community Builders works with a wide range of stakeholders, including residents, community organizations, government agencies, and businesses. They use a variety of tools and strategies to empower communities and build local capacity, including community organizing, capacity building, and community-based research.

While Community Builders is a passionate and dedicated organization, they face many challenges in achieving their mission. One of the biggest challenges they face is securing the funding they need to support their important work. Like many nonprofit organizations, Community Builders relies on a variety of funding sources, including individual donations, corporate sponsorships, and grants.

Grants are essential source of funding for Community Builders, as they provide the resources necessary to support their programs and initiatives. Grants enable Community Builders to invest in important community development initiatives, such as affordable housing, community health programs, and job training programs. These initiatives can have a significant impact on the lives of community members, helping to break the cycle of poverty and create a brighter future for all.

To achieve their goals through successful grant writing, Community Builders takes a strategic and intentional approach to identifying and applying for grants. They conduct thorough research to identify potential funders who share their mission and values, and who are interested in supporting their work. They also make sure to carefully review the requirements and guidelines for each grant opportunity, and tailor their proposals to fit the priorities and goals of the funder.

In their grant proposals, Community Builders places a strong emphasis on clearly articulating the need for their programs and initiatives. They provide data and evidence to demonstrate the impact of their work, and explain how their proposed programs will help to address the most pressing issues facing their communities. They also use compelling stories and real-world examples to bring their proposals to life, and demonstrate the real-world impact of their work.

Community Builders also places a strong emphasis on building strong relationships with their funders. They recognize that securing a grant is just the first step in a long-term partnership, and they work hard to cultivate and maintain strong relationships with their funders. They provide regular updates on their progress and achievements, and make sure to demonstrate their accountability and transparency in the use of the funds they receive.

Chapter 2
Identifying Potential Funding Sources

In order to secure funding for your nonprofit organization, it's essential to identify potential funding sources that align with your mission and values.

In this chapter, we'll discuss the key steps involved in identifying potential funding sources, including conducting research, building relationships with funders, and developing a strong understanding of the funding landscape.

Conducting Research

The first step in identifying potential funding sources is to conduct thorough research. There are a number of resources available to help you identify potential funders, including online databases, professional networks, and industry publications.

Online databases are an excellent resource for identifying potential funders. Many nonprofit organizations use databases such as Grant Station, Instrumentl or Foundation Directory Online to search for grants and other funding opportunities. These databases allow you to search for grants based on a wide range of criteria, including location, program area, and grant amount.

Professional networks are another valuable resource for identifying potential funders. Joining professional associations or attending industry conferences can help you connect with other nonprofit professionals and learn about funding opportunities that may be available.

Industry publications are also a useful resource for identifying potential funders. Many publications feature articles on grant opportunities and funding trends, and can provide valuable insights into the funding landscape in your field.

Building Relationships with Funders

Once you've identified potential funders, it's important to build strong relationships with them. Building relationships with funders can help you better understand their priorities and funding criteria, and can increase your chances of securing funding.

One way to build relationships with funders is to attend events and conferences where they are speaking or presenting. This can provide an opportunity to meet with funders, learn more about their work, and make a strong impression.

Another way to build relationships with funders is to engage with them on social media. Many funders have active social media accounts, and engaging with them on these platforms can help you build a rapport and demonstrate your interest in their work.

Finally, it's important to remember that building relationships with funders is a long-term process. You should be prepared to invest time and energy in building and maintaining relationships with funders, even if you don't receive funding from them right away.

Developing a Strong Understanding of the Funding Landscape

In addition to conducting research and building relationships with funders, it's important to develop a strong understanding of the funding landscape in your field. This can help you identify trends and opportunities that may not be immediately apparent, and can inform your approach to grant writing and fundraising.

One way to develop a strong understanding of the funding landscape is to research funding trends in your field. This can involve reading industry publications, attending conferences and events, and speaking with other nonprofit professionals. By understanding the funding trends in your field, you can better position your organization to secure funding and stay ahead of emerging opportunities.

It's also important to understand the funding priorities of individual funders. Each funder has its own priorities and criteria for awarding grants, and understanding these priorities can help you tailor your grant proposals to better align with their interests.

Finally, it's important to keep track of changes in the funding landscape over time. The funding landscape is constantly evolving, and it's important to stay up-to-date on new funding sources and trends that may emerge.

Identifying potential funding sources is an essential step in securing funding for your nonprofit organization. By conducting research, building relationships with funders, and developing a strong understanding of the funding landscape, you can increase your chances of securing funding and position your organization for long-term success. Remember, securing funding is a long-term process that requires ongoing research, engagement, and dedication. With the right approach, however, you can secure the resources you need to achieve your mission and make a positive impact in your community.

Creating a Database of Potential Funders

Once you have identified potential funders, it's important to create a database of potential funders. This can be as simple as an Excel spreadsheet, or a more complex system, such as a customer relationship management (CRM) platform. Your database should include key information about each funder, including their name, contact information, funding priorities, and requirements.

When creating your database, it's important to be thorough and organized. You should include all potential funders that meet your organization's funding priorities and requirements, even if you don't plan to apply to them immediately. You should also keep your database up-to-date, and remove funders that are no longer relevant, or add new ones as they become available.

Using Grant Search Engines

Grant search engines are another useful tool for researching grant opportunities. These platforms allow you to search for grants based on a wide range of criteria, including location, program area, and grant amount. Many grant search engines are free, and can be a useful resource for identifying new funding opportunities.

Some popular grant search engines include GrantWatch, Grants.gov, and GrantStation. It's important to remember that while grant search engines can be a valuable tool, they should not be relied on exclusively. It's important to conduct additional research on potential funders to ensure that they align with your organization's mission and values, and to understand their specific funding priorities and requirements.

In summary, researching grant opportunities is a critical step in the grant writing process. By conducting thorough research, creating a database of potential funders, and using grant search engines to identify new funding opportunities, you can increase your chances of securing funding for your nonprofit organization. Remember, securing funding is a long-term process that requires ongoing research, engagement, and dedication. With the right approach, however, you can secure the resources you need to achieve your mission and make a positive impact in your community.

Understanding Grant Guidelines and Requirements

In order to successfully apply for and receive grant funding, it's important to thoroughly understand the grant guidelines and requirements set forth by potential funders. In this chapter, we will discuss the key components of grant guidelines, how to interpret them, and strategies for meeting the requirements of potential funders.

Key Components of Grant Guidelines

Grant guidelines are a set of instructions and requirements that potential funders provide to applicants. They outline the specific criteria and requirements for applying for and receiving grant funding, and typically include information on eligibility, funding priorities, application deadlines, and reporting requirements.

Eligibility

One of the most important components of grant guidelines is eligibility. This section outlines the specific criteria that potential applicants must meet in order to be eligible for funding. This may include requirements related to the type of organization, the geographic location of the organization, or the types of programs or projects that the organization operates.

Funding Priorities

Grant guidelines also typically include information on the funding priorities of potential funders. This section outlines the types of programs or projects that funders are interested in supporting, and can provide valuable insights into the types of programs or projects that are most likely to receive funding.

Application Deadlines

Grant guidelines also typically include information on application deadlines. This section outlines the specific dates by which applications must be submitted, as well as any other important deadlines or milestones in the application process.

Reporting Requirements

Finally, grant guidelines typically include information on reporting requirements. This section outlines the specific types of reports and other documentation that grantees must submit in order to maintain funding, as well as any other requirements related to ongoing monitoring and evaluation.

Interpreting Grant Guidelines

Once you have identified potential funders and obtained their grant guidelines, it's important to interpret them carefully. This involves reviewing the guidelines in detail, and identifying any areas where your organization may need to make adjustments in order to meet the requirements of the funder.

One of the most important aspects of interpreting grant guidelines is understanding the funding priorities of the funder. This can help you tailor your application to the specific interests and priorities of the funder, and increase your chances of receiving funding.

It's also important to carefully review the eligibility requirements outlined in the grant guidelines. If your organization does not meet the eligibility requirements, it's unlikely that you will be considered for funding. However, if you are unsure whether or not your organization meets the eligibility requirements, it's worth reaching out to the funder to ask for clarification.

Finally, it's important to carefully review the reporting requirements outlined in the grant guidelines. This can help you prepare for the ongoing monitoring and evaluation that will be required if your organization receives funding, and can help you ensure that you are prepared to meet the funder's requirements.

Strategies for Meeting Grant Requirements

In order to successfully meet the requirements of potential funders, there are several strategies that your organization can employ.

First, it's important to carefully tailor your application to the specific interests and priorities of the funder. This may involve highlighting specific aspects of your organization's work that align with the funder's funding priorities, or emphasizing specific outcomes or impacts that the funder is interested in supporting.

Second, it's important to be thorough and accurate in your application. This means carefully reviewing the application guidelines and requirements, and ensuring that your application meets all of the necessary criteria. It's also important to provide accurate and detailed information about your organization and its programs or projects.

Third, it's important to be prepared to meet the ongoing reporting and evaluation requirements of the funder. This may involve developing a system for tracking and reporting on key performance indicators, or conducting regular evaluations of your organization's programs or projects.

In summary, understanding grant guidelines and requirements is a critical component of the grant writing process. By carefully interpreting grant guidelines and tailoring your application to the specific interests and priorities of potential funders, your organization can increase its chances of successfully securing grant funding. Additionally, being prepared to meet the ongoing reporting and evaluation requirements of funders can help ensure that your organization maintains funding and continues to make progress towards its goals.

It's also important to remember that grant guidelines and requirements can vary significantly from funder to funder. As a result, it's important to carefully review the guidelines and requirements for each potential funder that your organization is considering, and to tailor your application and reporting strategies accordingly.

More so, it's worth noting that grant guidelines and requirements are subject to change over time. As a result, it's important to stay up-to-date on any changes or updates to the guidelines and requirements of potential funders, and to adjust your strategies and applications accordingly.

In order to effectively research and interpret grant guidelines and requirements, there are several steps that your organization can take. These include:

1. **Identify potential funders**: The first step in the process is to identify potential funders that align with your organization's mission and goals. This may involve conducting research online, attending grant writing workshops or conferences, or networking with other nonprofit organizations.
2. **Obtain grant guidelines**: Once you have identified potential funders, it's important to obtain their grant guidelines. These can typically be found on the funder's website, or by contacting the funder directly.
3. **Review the guidelines in detail**: Once you have obtained the grant guidelines, it's important to review them in detail. This may involve taking notes, highlighting key sections, or developing a checklist to ensure that your application meets all of the necessary criteria.
4. **Tailor your application**: Based on your interpretation of the grant guidelines, it's important to tailor your application to the specific interests and priorities of the funder. This may involve highlighting specific aspects of your

organization's work, or emphasizing specific outcomes or impacts that the funder is interested in supporting.

5. **Prepare for ongoing reporting and evaluation**: Finally, it's important to be prepared to meet the ongoing reporting and evaluation requirements of the funder. This may involve developing a system for tracking and reporting on key performance indicators, or conducting regular evaluations of your organization's programs or projects.

Evaluating the fit between your Nonprofit and Potential Funders

One of the most important aspects of successful grant writing is ensuring that there is a good fit between your nonprofit and potential funders. By evaluating this fit early on in the process, your organization can save time and resources and increase your chances of securing funding.

In order to evaluate the fit between your nonprofit and potential funders, there are several key factors to consider:

1. **Mission Alignment:** One of the most important factors to consider when evaluating the fit between your nonprofit and potential funders is mission alignment. This involves examining the funder's mission and goals, as well as their past giving history, to determine if their interests and priorities align with those of your organization.

2. **Programmatic Alignment**: In addition to mission alignment, it's important to consider whether there is programmatic alignment between your nonprofit and potential funders. This involves examining the specific programs and projects that your organization is proposing, and determining if they align with the priorities and funding interests of the potential funder.

3. **Geographic Focus**: Another important factor to consider when evaluating the fit between your nonprofit and

potential funders is geographic focus. Some funders may have a specific focus on a particular geographic region or community, and may only consider proposals from organizations working in those areas.

4. **Funding Level**: It's also important to consider the funding level that the potential funder is offering, and whether this aligns with your organization's needs and goals. Some funders may offer smaller grants that are more suitable for specific programs or projects, while others may offer larger grants that can support broader organizational goals.

5. **Application Process**: Finally, it's important to consider the application process for each potential funder, and whether your organization has the capacity and resources to meet the application requirements. Some funders may require detailed reports, extensive financial documentation, or other materials that can be time-consuming and resource-intensive to produce.

By evaluating these factors early on in the grant writing process, your organization can identify potential funders that are a good fit for your mission, programs, and goals. This can save time and resources by focusing your efforts on funders that are most likely to be interested in supporting your organization, and can increase your chances of successfully securing grant funding.

It's worth noting that evaluating the fit between your nonprofit and potential funders is an ongoing process, and should be revisited regularly as your organization's programs and priorities evolve. By staying attuned to changes in the funding landscape and the evolving needs of your organization, you can continue to identify new funding opportunities and build strong relationships with potential funders over time.

CASE STUDY

To build on the hypothetical nonprofit introduced in Chapter 1, let's say that the organization is a youth-focused nonprofit that provides after-school programming to underprivileged children in urban areas. The organization's programs include academic tutoring, mentorship, and enrichment activities like sports and art classes. The nonprofit is seeking funding to expand their programming and serve more children in their community.

In this section, we will research several real-world grant opportunities that could be a good fit for this nonprofit, and provide examples of how the nonprofit could tailor their proposal to each funder's specific guidelines and requirements.

1. The Charles Stewart Mott Foundation

The Charles Stewart Mott Foundation is a private foundation that supports a wide range of nonprofit organizations, with a focus on empowering people and communities. The Foundation's Youth and Education program provides funding for programs that improve educational outcomes for young people, with a specific focus on low-income and underserved communities. For our hypothetical nonprofit, this could be a great funding opportunity, given their focus on providing after-school programming to underprivileged children. To tailor their proposal to the Foundation's guidelines, the nonprofit would want to emphasize how their programs align with the Foundation's priorities and funding interests. This could include highlighting their focus on academic tutoring and mentorship, as well as their commitment to serving children in urban areas. In addition, the nonprofit would want to make sure they are familiar with the Foundation's application process, which includes submitting a letter of inquiry before being invited to submit a full proposal.

2. The William T. Grant Foundation

The William T. Grant Foundation is a private foundation that funds research and programs that improve the lives of young people. The Foundation's Youth Service Improvement Grants provide funding for organizations that are seeking to improve the quality of youth services in their communities. For our hypothetical nonprofit, this funding opportunity could be a good fit, given their focus on providing high-quality after-school programming to underprivileged children. To tailor their proposal to the Foundation's guidelines, the nonprofit would want to emphasize their commitment to program quality, including the use of evidence-based practices and regular program evaluation. In addition, they would want to highlight their focus on serving low-income and underprivileged children in urban areas. As part of the application process, the Foundation requires a letter of inquiry and a proposal narrative, which provides an opportunity for the nonprofit to highlight their program's impact and potential for improvement.

3. The U.S. Department of Education - 21st Century Community Learning Centers Program

The U.S. Department of Education's 21st Century Community Learning Centers program provides funding for organizations that offer before- and after-school programs to students in high-poverty and low-performing schools. This program could be a great funding opportunity for our hypothetical nonprofit, given their focus on providing after-school programming to underprivileged children. To tailor their proposal to the Department of

Education's guidelines, the nonprofit would want to emphasize their focus on academic tutoring and enrichment activities, which aligns with the program's goals of improving students' academic achievement and providing safe and supportive learning environments. In addition, the nonprofit would want to make sure they are familiar with the program's strict guidelines and requirements, which include a focus on evidence-based practices, regular program evaluation, and partnership with local schools and community organizations.

4. The National Endowment for the Arts - Arts Education Grant Program

While our hypothetical nonprofit's focus is primarily on academic tutoring and enrichment activities, they may also offer arts programming to their students. If this is the case, the National Endowment for the Arts' Arts Education Grant Program could be a good fit. This program provides funding for arts education programs that serve K-12 students, with a focus on reaching underserved populations. To tailor their proposal to the Endowment's guidelines, the nonprofit would want to emphasize the role that arts programming

The National Endowment for the Arts (NEA) is a federal agency that provides funding to support the arts and artistic projects in the United States. The NEA supports a wide range of arts-related activities, including dance, music, theater, literature, visual arts, and interdisciplinary projects.

One of the NEA's primary grant programs is the Art Works program, which provides funding for projects that promote artistic excellence and public engagement with the arts. The Art Works program is divided into three categories: Art Works I, Art Works II, and Art Works III. Art Works I grants support projects that focus on the creation of art and the presentation of art to the public. Art Works II grants support projects that focus on the national or regional distribution of art, and Art Works III grants support projects that focus on engaging the public with the arts.

In addition to the Art Works program, the NEA offers a number of other grant programs that support specific artistic disciplines and initiatives. For example, the NEA offers grants to support arts education, folk and traditional arts, local arts agencies, and creative placemaking projects. The NEA also offers grants to support projects that promote access to the arts for underserved populations, such as veterans, people with disabilities, and people living in rural communities.

When considering applying for an NEA grant, it's important to carefully review the guidelines and requirements for the specific program you are interested in. The NEA provides detailed information about each grant program on their website, including eligibility requirements, application instructions, and review criteria.

To tailor a proposal to the NEA's guidelines and requirements, it's important to thoroughly research the specific program and understand what the NEA is looking for in a successful grant application. For example, the NEA places a strong emphasis on artistic excellence, so it's important to clearly demonstrate the artistic merit of your proposed project and how it will contribute to the artistic landscape in the United States. It's also important to provide a detailed project budget that clearly outlines how the grant funds will be used, and to demonstrate a strong plan for promoting public engagement with the arts.

Overall, the National Endowment for the Arts offers a wide range of grant opportunities for nonprofit organizations and individuals working in the arts. By carefully researching the available grant programs and tailoring your proposal to the NEA's guidelines and requirements, your nonprofit can increase its chances of receiving funding to support its important artistic projects and initiatives.

Chapter 3
Preparing to write a Grant

Preparing to write a grant proposal is a critical step in the grant writing process. It involves a thorough analysis of your nonprofit's needs and goals, as well as a detailed understanding of the grant program you are applying to.

In this chapter, we will explore some of the key steps in preparing to write a successful grant proposal.

1. **Analyze your nonprofit's needs and goals:** The first step in preparing to write a grant proposal is to analyze your nonprofit's needs and goals. This involves identifying the specific program or project you wish to fund, as well as the outcomes you hope to achieve through the grant funding. You should also consider the resources your nonprofit has available, including staff, volunteers, and other funding sources.

2. **Research the grant program**: Once you have a clear understanding of your nonprofit's needs and goals, the next step is to research the grant program you are applying to. This involves carefully reviewing the program guidelines and requirements, as well as any relevant application materials. You should also research the funding history of the grant program, as well as the priorities and values of the funding organization.

3. **Develop a project plan**: Based on your nonprofit's needs and goals, as well as the requirements of the grant program, you should develop a detailed project plan. This plan should outline the specific activities and milestones that your nonprofit will undertake with the grant funding, as well as the timeline and budget for the project. It should

also clearly demonstrate how the project aligns with the priorities and goals of the funding organization.

4. **Assemble a grant writing team:** Preparing a successful grant proposal often requires a team effort. You should assemble a team of staff and volunteers who will be responsible for developing and submitting the grant proposal. This team should include individuals with expertise in the program or project area, as well as individuals with strong writing and research skills.

5. **Gather necessary information and materials:** To prepare a successful grant proposal, you will need to gather a range of information and materials. This may include financial statements, organizational documents, resumes of key staff members, letters of support from community partners, and other relevant materials. It is important to carefully review the grant program guidelines to ensure that you are including all necessary information in your proposal.

6. **Identify potential challenges and develop solutions:** As part of your preparation process, it is important to identify potential challenges that may arise during the grant writing and implementation process. This may include challenges related to budget constraints, staffing and resource limitations, and unforeseen obstacles that may arise during the project. Once you have identified potential challenges, you should develop solutions to address these challenges, and include them in your project plan.

7. **Develop a budget:** A key component of any successful grant proposal is a well-developed budget. Your budget should outline the costs associated with your project, including personnel, equipment, supplies, and other expenses. You should also clearly identify any matching funds or in-kind contributions that your nonprofit will be providing, as well as any other sources of funding that you will be seeking to support the project. Your budget should

be realistic and align with the guidelines and requirements of the grant program.

8. **Establish a timeline**: In addition to a budget, a detailed timeline is an important component of your grant proposal. Your timeline should clearly outline the key activities and milestones associated with your project, including start and end dates, major deliverables, and key deadlines. Your timeline should be realistic and reflect the needs and resources of your nonprofit, as well as the requirements of the grant program.

9. **Review and revise**: Once you have completed your project plan, assembled your grant writing team, gathered all necessary information and materials, and developed a budget and timeline, it is important to review and revise your proposal before submitting it. This should include a careful review of all application materials to ensure that you have addressed all of the program guidelines and requirements, as well as a review of the proposal for clarity, coherence, and relevance to the funding organization's priorities and goals. It can also be helpful to have a peer review process, where someone outside of your team reviews the proposal for any areas that may need improvement.

Organizing your Team and Resources

Organizing your team and resources is a critical component of successful grant writing. By assembling a team that is knowledgeable about your nonprofit's mission and goals, as well as the grant program you are applying for, and gathering all necessary resources and materials, you can increase your chances of success.

1. **Identify your grant writing team**: The first step in organizing your team is to identify the individuals who will be responsible for developing and submitting the grant

proposal. This may include staff members, board members, volunteers, or consultants with expertise in grant writing or the specific program area. It is important to select individuals who have a deep understanding of your nonprofit's mission and goals, and who can work collaboratively to develop a strong proposal.

2. **Define roles and responsibilities**: Once you have identified your grant writing team, it is important to define roles and responsibilities. This may include assigning individuals to lead various aspects of the proposal development process, such as research, writing, budget development, and program design. Clearly defining roles and responsibilities can help ensure that everyone is working towards a common goal and that there is a shared understanding of what is expected.

3. **Establish a timeline and milestones**: As part of your team organization process, you should establish a timeline and milestones for the grant proposal development process. This timeline should include key deadlines for gathering information, writing, budget development, and review and revision. It can be helpful to create a project plan or Gantt chart to visualize the timeline and ensure that everyone is aware of key deadlines and milestones.

4. **Gather necessary resources and materials**: In addition to assembling a strong grant writing team, it is important to gather all necessary resources and materials to support the development of the proposal. This may include financial reports, program evaluations, and other documentation related to your nonprofit's activities and achievements. It may also include research on the grant program and its priorities and requirements.

5. **Establish communication protocols**: Effective communication is critical to the success of any grant writing team. As part of your team organization process, you should establish communication protocols, including regular meetings or check-ins, and clear expectations for

how information will be shared and disseminated. This can help ensure that everyone is on the same page and that there is a shared understanding of the proposal development process.

6. **Define the project scope and goals:** Before you begin writing the proposal, it is important to define the project scope and goals. This may involve a needs assessment or analysis of your nonprofit's existing programs and services, as well as an evaluation of the goals and priorities of the grant program. By defining the project scope and goals, you can ensure that your proposal is targeted, focused, and aligned with the funding organization's priorities.

7. **Develop a project plan and budget**: As you prepare to write the proposal, it is important to develop a detailed project plan and budget. This plan should include specific objectives, activities, and timelines for the proposed project, as well as a detailed budget that outlines the costs associated with each activity or objective. Developing a clear project plan and budget can help ensure that your proposal is well-organized and aligned with the priorities and requirements of the funding organization.

8. **Utilize project management tools**: Effective project management is critical to the success of any grant proposal. To ensure that your team is working efficiently and effectively, consider utilizing project management tools such as project management software or a shared project folder. These tools can help you track progress, share information, and ensure that everyone is aware of key deadlines and milestones.

9. **Establish a review process**: Once you have developed a draft proposal, it is important to establish a review process to ensure that the proposal is well-written, well-organized, and effectively communicates your nonprofit's mission and goals. This may involve assigning specific individuals to review and provide feedback on different sections of the proposal, or conducting a full team review of the proposal.

By establishing a review process, you can ensure that your proposal is polished and well-prepared before submission.

10. **Practice effective time management**: Finally, effective time management is critical to the success of any grant writing team. To ensure that your team is working efficiently and effectively, consider establishing a regular meeting schedule, setting clear expectations for deadlines and milestones, and utilizing time management tools such as to-do lists or project management software. By practicing effective time management, you can help ensure that your proposal is completed on time and to the best of your team's abilities.

Overall, organizing your team and resources is a critical component of successful grant writing.

By following these tips, you can increase your chances of success and ensure that your proposal is well-prepared, well-informed, and effectively communicates your nonprofit's mission and goals to the funding organization.

Developing a Project Plan and Budget

Developing a project plan and budget is a critical component of successful grant writing. By creating a clear, detailed plan and budget, you can demonstrate to funders that you have a well-organized and effective plan for achieving your project goals.

Here are some key tips for developing a project plan and budget:

1. **Identify project goals and objectives**: Before you begin developing your project plan and budget, it's important to identify your project goals and objectives. What do you

hope to achieve through your proposed project? What specific activities and outcomes do you anticipate? By defining your goals and objectives up front, you can ensure that your project plan and budget are well-aligned with your overall project vision.

2. **Break down project activities into specific tasks**: Once you have identified your project goals and objectives, it's important to break down the project activities into specific tasks. What specific steps will be necessary to achieve your project goals and objectives? By breaking down the project activities into specific tasks, you can ensure that your project plan and budget are well-organized and easy to understand.

3. **Estimate the time and resources required for each task**: Once you have identified the specific tasks required to achieve your project goals and objectives, it's important to estimate the time and resources required for each task. How long will each task take? What resources will be required (such as staff time, materials, or equipment)? By estimating the time and resources required for each task, you can ensure that your project plan and budget are realistic and well-informed.

4. **Develop a timeline for the project**: Once you have estimated the time and resources required for each task, it's important to develop a timeline for the project. When will each task take place? What are the key milestones and deadlines for the project? By developing a clear timeline, you can ensure that your project plan and budget are well-organized and aligned with the funding organization's expectations.

5. **Develop a detailed budget**: Finally, it's important to develop a detailed budget for your proposed project. This budget should include all of the costs associated with each task, including staff time, materials, equipment, and other expenses. Be sure to include both direct costs (such as salaries and supplies) and indirect costs (such as overhead

and administrative expenses). By developing a detailed budget, you can demonstrate to funders that you have a clear and well-organized plan for utilizing their funds.

. By following these tips, you can ensure that your project plan and budget are well-organized, well-informed, and effectively communicate your nonprofit's mission and goals to the funding organization.

Defining Project Goals and Objectives

Defining project goals and objectives is a crucial step in developing a successful grant proposal. Without clear goals and objectives, it can be difficult to communicate your project's purpose and desired outcomes to potential funders.

In this chapter, we'll discuss the importance of defining project goals and objectives, how to develop them, and some tips to make sure they are well-written and effective.

Why are project goals and objectives important?

Project goals and objectives provide a clear framework for what you want to accomplish with your project.

Goals are broad statements that describe the overall purpose of the project, while objectives are specific and measurable steps that are taken to achieve those goals.

By defining your goals and objectives, you are able to establish clear expectations for what your project will accomplish and how you will measure success.

In addition to providing a framework for your project, having well-defined goals and objectives also helps you communicate the value of your project to potential funders. Grant reviewers want to see that your project is well-planned and has a clear purpose. They want to understand how your project will impact your community, and what specific outcomes you hope to achieve. Well-defined goals and objectives help make your proposal stand out by demonstrating that you have a clear plan and are committed to achieving tangible results.

How to develop project goals and objectives:

When developing project goals and objectives, it's important to be specific, measurable, achievable, relevant, and time-bound. These criteria are commonly referred to as **SMART goals**.

Here's a breakdown of what each letter stands for:

- **Specific:** Your goals and objectives should be clear and specific, avoiding vague language or broad generalizations. You should be able to clearly articulate what you hope to achieve.
- **Measurable**: Your goals and objectives should be quantifiable, so that you can track your progress and determine whether you have achieved your desired outcomes.
- **Achievable**: Your goals and objectives should be realistic and achievable, based on your available resources and timeline.
- **Relevant**: Your goals and objectives should align with your organization's mission and values, and be relevant to the needs of your community.
- **Time-bound:** Your goals and objectives should have a specific timeline for achievement.

To develop effective project goals and objectives, start by identifying your project's overarching goal. This could be something like "To improve the literacy rates of children in our community."

Once you have your goal, break it down into specific, measurable objectives that will help you achieve it.

For example, one objective could be "To provide after-school tutoring to 100 elementary school students in our community by the end of the school year."

Tips for writing effective project goals and objectives

Here are a few tips to keep in mind as you write your project goals and objectives:

1. **Be specific**: Your goals and objectives should be clear and specific, avoiding vague or broad statements. Use concrete language and measurable criteria to define what you want to achieve.
2. **Be realistic**: While it's important to aim high, your goals and objectives should also be achievable within the scope of your resources and timeframe. Be honest about what is feasible for your organization.
3. **Be relevant:** Ensure that your goals and objectives are relevant to your organization's mission and the needs of the community you serve. Consider how your project will impact the community and how it aligns with your organization's values and goals.
4. **Be measurable:** Make sure that you have a way to measure progress and success towards your goals and objectives. This will allow you to track your progress and make any necessary adjustments as you go.
5. **Use action-oriented language:** Use action verbs to describe what you plan to do and how you plan to achieve

your goals and objectives. This will help to clarify the steps that need to be taken and create a sense of momentum.

6. **Involve your team**: Engage your team in the process of developing project goals and objectives. This will ensure that everyone is on the same page and has a shared understanding of the project's purpose and goals.

7. **Get feedback**: Seek input and feedback from stakeholders, such as community members, partners, and funders. This can help you to refine your goals and objectives and ensure that they are relevant and impactful.

By following these tips and using the SMART criteria, you can develop clear and effective project goals and objectives that will help you create a strong and compelling grant proposal. Remember, your goals and objectives are the backbone of your project, and are crucial to demonstrating to funders that you have a clear plan and are committed to achieving measurable results.

In addition to the tips mentioned above, it's also important to involve your team in the process of developing project goals and objectives. By collaborating with your team, you can ensure that everyone is on the same page and that you have buy-in from all stakeholders.

Here are a few steps you can take to involve your team in developing project goals and objectives:

1. **Schedule a team meeting**: Set aside time to meet with your team to discuss your project goals and objectives. This can be done in person or virtually.

2. **Brainstorm ideas**: Ask your team to brainstorm ideas for specific, measurable objectives that will help you achieve your project goals. Encourage everyone to share their ideas, and avoid dismissing any suggestions out of hand.

3. **Evaluate ideas**: Once you have a list of objectives, evaluate them based on the SMART criteria. Are they specific, measurable, achievable, relevant, and time-bound? If not, see if you can revise them to make them more effective.
4. **Refine and prioritize**: Refine your objectives based on feedback from your team and any other stakeholders, and prioritize them based on their importance to your project's overall success.
5. **Finalize your goals and objectives:** Once you have a list of well-defined goals and objectives, finalize them and ensure that everyone on your team understands and supports them.

By involving your team in the process of developing project goals and objectives, you can ensure that everyone is invested in the project's success and has a clear understanding of what needs to be accomplished. This can help foster a sense of teamwork and collaboration, and can also lead to better outcomes for your project.

In addition to involving your team, it's also important to consider how you will measure progress towards your project goals and objectives. By including specific, measurable metrics in your proposal, you can demonstrate to funders that you have a clear plan for evaluating your project's success. This can include things like the number of people served, the percentage of participants who achieve specific outcomes, or other quantitative measures that align with your project's goals.

By defining project goals and objectives that are specific, measurable, achievable, relevant, and time-bound, and by involving your team in the process, you can create a strong and compelling grant proposal that demonstrates your commitment to achieving tangible results. Remember, your goals and objectives are a key component of your proposal, and are essential to helping funders understand the value of your project and its potential impact on your community.

CASE STUDY

Let's take a look at a hypothetical case study of a nonprofit organization that successfully developed a grant proposal through effective planning and teamwork.

The organization is called "Green Horizons," a nonprofit dedicated to promoting sustainable living practices in their community. Their mission is to raise awareness about environmental issues and provide education and resources to individuals and families to help them reduce their carbon footprint and live more sustainably.

After conducting research and identifying several potential grant opportunities, the organization decided to apply for a grant from the Green Initiatives Foundation, a foundation that supports environmental initiatives in communities across the country.

To begin, Green Horizons assembled a diverse team of staff and volunteers, including individuals with expertise in environmental education, community outreach, and grant writing. The team worked together to develop a detailed project plan that aligned with the priorities of the Green Initiatives Foundation and would help them achieve their mission.

The project plan included a series of workshops that would educate participants on topics such as composting, sustainable gardening, and energy efficiency. In addition, the organization planned to create a "Green Living Toolkit," which would provide participants with resources and tools to help them implement sustainable practices in their daily lives.

To support these efforts, Green Horizons developed a detailed project budget that accounted for all necessary expenses, including materials for the workshops, staff and volunteer time, and marketing and outreach materials.

One of the keys to the organization's success was their ability to align their goals with the funder's priorities. The Green Initiatives Foundation had a specific focus on promoting sustainable living practices among low-income communities, which was also a key priority for Green Horizons. The organization was able to demonstrate how their project would address this priority by targeting low-income neighborhoods and providing free workshops and resources to participants.

In addition, Green Horizons emphasized the potential impact of their project in their grant proposal, highlighting the potential for reducing carbon emissions, improving air and water quality, and promoting healthier and more sustainable lifestyles for community members.

The team worked diligently to craft a well-written and compelling grant proposal that effectively communicated their mission, goals, and project plan to the Green Initiatives Foundation. The proposal was supported by a strong project budget, a detailed timeline, and testimonials from community members and other partners who had worked with Green Horizons in the past.

After submitting the proposal, Green Horizons was thrilled to receive notification that their proposal had been accepted, and they were awarded the grant from the Green Initiatives Foundation.

By organizing a diverse team, developing a detailed project plan and budget, and aligning their goals with the funder's priorities, Green Horizons was able to successfully develop a grant proposal that secured funding for their important work promoting sustainable living practices in their community. This case study highlights the importance of effective planning and teamwork in grant writing, and the value of aligning your goals with the priorities of potential funders.

Chapter 4
Writing the Grant Proposal

In this chapter, we will discuss the key components of a successful grant proposal and provide tips and strategies for crafting a compelling and persuasive application.

1. **The Executive Summary:** The executive summary is the first section of your grant proposal, and it provides an overview of your project and its goals. The executive summary should be concise, compelling, and engaging, and it should clearly outline the purpose of the project and why it is important.
2. **Introduction**: The introduction of your grant proposal provides an opportunity to introduce your organization and its mission to the funder. It should be written in a clear, concise, and compelling way, and it should provide background information about the project.
3. **Problem Statement**: The problem statement is a crucial component of your grant proposal. It should provide a clear and concise description of the problem that your project aims to address. The problem statement should be backed up by data and statistics to provide evidence that the problem exists.
4. **Goals and Objectives**: The goals and objectives section of your grant proposal should describe the specific outcomes that you hope to achieve through your project. Your goals and objectives should be specific, measurable, achievable, relevant, and time-bound (SMART). Make sure that your goals and objectives align with the funder's priorities and guidelines.

5. **Methods and Activities:** The methods and activities section of your grant proposal should describe the specific strategies and activities that you will use to achieve your goals and objectives. It should provide a clear and concise description of the steps that you will take to implement your project.

6. **Evaluation**: The evaluation section of your grant proposal should describe how you will measure the success of your project. It should include specific metrics and targets that you will use to track progress toward your goals and objectives. Make sure that your evaluation plan aligns with the funder's requirements.

7. **Budget:** The budget section of your grant proposal should provide a detailed breakdown of the costs associated with your project. It should include a line-item budget that outlines all expenses, as well as a narrative that explains the rationale for each expense. Make sure that your budget aligns with the funder's requirements and guidelines.

8. **Conclusion**: The conclusion of your grant proposal should summarize the key points of your proposal and reiterate the importance of your project. It should be written in a clear and compelling way, and it should provide a sense of urgency and importance to the funder.

Tips for Writing a Successful Grant Proposal

1. **Research the Funder**: Before you start writing your grant proposal, make sure that you research the funder to understand their priorities and guidelines. This will help you tailor your proposal to the funder's specific requirements and increase your chances of success.

2. **Be Clear and Concise**: Your grant proposal should be written in a clear and concise way that is easy to understand. Avoid using jargon or technical language that might be confusing to the reader.

3. **Use Data and Statistics:** Use data and statistics to support your problem statement and goals and objectives. This will help to provide evidence that the problem exists and increase the credibility of your proposal.
4. **Be Realistic**: Make sure that your goals and objectives are realistic and achievable. Don't over-promise and under-deliver, as this will damage your credibility and reduce your chances of future funding.
5. **Align with the Funder's Priorities**: Make sure that your project aligns with the funder's priorities and guidelines. This will increase the relevance of your proposal and make it more likely to be successful.
6. **Get Feedback**: Before submitting your grant proposal, get feedback from colleagues, volunteers, and others who are familiar with your project. This will help you identify areas for improvement and increase the overall quality of your proposal.

In summary, writing a grant proposal requires careful planning, research, and attention to detail. You should take the time to develop a project plan and budget, as well as a persuasive and clear proposal that demonstrates the value and impact of your project. By following these tips, you can increase your chances of success and secure the funding you need to make a difference in your community.

Crafting a Compelling Narrative

When it comes to writing a grant proposal, it's not just about presenting data and facts. It's important to tell a compelling story that engages the reader and conveys your organization's mission and goals. Crafting a narrative that resonates with funders can be a challenge, but it's a crucial part of the grant writing process.

Here are some tips for crafting a compelling narrative:

1. **Start with a hook**: The beginning of your proposal should grab the reader's attention and draw them in. Consider starting with a powerful statistic or anecdote that highlights the problem your organization is working to solve.
2. **Use storytelling techniques**: Incorporate storytelling techniques into your proposal, such as case studies or personal anecdotes that illustrate the impact of your work. People connect with stories, and they can help funders understand the real-world impact of your organization's work.
3. **Be clear and concise**: While you want to tell a story, you also need to be clear and concise. Avoid getting bogged down in unnecessary details, and make sure your narrative is focused on the key points you want to convey.
4. **Highlight the human element**: People want to support causes that help other people. Make sure your narrative emphasizes the human element of your organization's work, and how it improves the lives of those it serves.
5. **Make a connection:** When crafting your narrative, think about what will resonate with the funder. What are their values and priorities? How does your work align with those priorities? Making a connection with the funder can help your proposal stand out and increase your chances of success.
6. **Use active voice**: Using active voice can help your narrative feel more engaging and impactful. Instead of writing "the problem was addressed by our organization," write "our organization addressed the problem." It may seem like a small change, but it can make a big difference in how your narrative is received.
7. **Focus on the future:** While it's important to highlight the impact your organization has had in the past, don't forget to focus on the future. Funders want to know that their

investment will make a difference, and that your organization has a clear plan for how to achieve its goals.

In summary, crafting a compelling narrative is essential for writing a successful grant proposal. Use storytelling techniques, be clear and concise, highlight the human element, make a connection with the funder, use active voice, and focus on the future. By following these tips, you can create a narrative that resonates with funders and helps your organization secure the funding it needs to achieve its goals.

Meeting Funder Expectations and Guidelines

When it comes to grant writing, one of the most important aspects to keep in mind is meeting the expectations and guidelines set forth by the funder.

This is because funders have specific criteria that they are looking for in grant proposals, and failing to meet these criteria can result in a rejection of the proposal. In this chapter, we will explore how to meet funder expectations and guidelines when writing a grant proposal.

The first step in meeting funder expectations and guidelines is to carefully review the guidelines and instructions provided by the funder.

Make sure that you understand what the funder is looking for in a proposal, and what they are not looking for. Pay close attention to the formatting and submission requirements, as well as any specific information that the funder requests in the proposal.

Some funders may require a specific format, such as a certain font size or margin size, and failing to adhere to these requirements can result in disqualification.

In addition to reviewing the guidelines and instructions, it is important to research the funder and understand their mission, values, and priorities. This will help you to tailor your proposal to the funder's interests and make it more likely that your proposal will be accepted. You may also be able to find examples of successful proposals that have been submitted to the funder in the past, which can give you an idea of what the funder is looking for in a proposal.

When crafting your proposal, be sure to address each of the funder's requirements and guidelines. Use the same terminology and language that the funder uses in their guidelines, and be sure to provide all of the information that the funder requests. You should also make sure that your proposal is well-organized and easy to read. Use headings and subheadings to break up the text and make it easy for the funder to follow the flow of the proposal.

Another important aspect of meeting funder expectations and guidelines is to be honest and transparent in your proposal. Do not exaggerate or make false claims in your proposal, as this can lead to a rejection of your proposal and damage your organization's reputation. Instead, be clear and concise in your proposal, and provide supporting evidence to back up your claims.

In addition to the written content of your proposal, it is also important to include any required attachments, such as budgets, financial statements, and letters of support. Make sure that these attachments are organized and clearly labeled, and that they adhere to the funder's requirements.

Finally, be sure to proofread your proposal carefully before submitting it. Typos and grammatical errors can make your proposal appear unprofessional, and may cause the funder to question your attention to detail. Have someone else read over your proposal as well, to catch any errors that you may have missed.

Creating a Realistic Project Budget

When it comes to writing a grant proposal, one of the key components is creating a realistic project budget. This budget serves as a financial plan that outlines how the grant funds will be allocated to achieve the proposed project goals and objectives.

A well-crafted budget can increase the likelihood of securing a grant, as funders want to ensure that their investments will be used effectively and efficiently. In this chapter, we will discuss some important tips for creating a realistic project budget that will meet funder expectations and requirements.

1. Determine the Total Cost of the Project

The first step in creating a project budget is to determine the total cost of the project. This includes all the expenses related to the project, such as personnel, equipment, materials, and any other costs that may be associated with the project.

It is important to be as comprehensive as possible in identifying all expenses, so that the budget accurately reflects the total cost of the project. It may be helpful to use a spreadsheet or budgeting software to organize the information and ensure that nothing is overlooked.

2. Allocate Funds Appropriately

Once you have determined the total cost of the project, the next step is to allocate the funds appropriately. This involves breaking down the total cost into specific categories or line items, such as personnel, equipment, materials, and so on.

It is important to allocate funds in a way that aligns with the project goals and objectives, and also meets funder requirements. Some funders may have specific guidelines or limitations on how grant funds can be used, so it is important to carefully review the guidelines and requirements to ensure that the budget is in line with funder expectations.

3. Use Realistic Costs

When creating a project budget, it is important to use realistic costs for each line item. This includes taking into account the current market prices for materials and equipment, as well as reasonable estimates for personnel costs and other expenses.

It is also important to account for any unforeseen expenses or unexpected costs that may arise during the project. This can be done by including a contingency fund or by allocating some funds to a separate category for unexpected expenses.

4. Ensure the Budget is Easy to Understand

It is important to ensure that the project budget is easy to understand and clearly outlines how the grant funds will be allocated. This can be done by using clear and concise language, and by breaking down the budget into specific categories or line items.

Additionally, it may be helpful to include explanatory notes or annotations that provide additional context or detail on specific line items. This can help funders better understand how the grant funds will be used, and increase the likelihood of securing the grant.

5. Have the Budget Reviewed

Finally, it is a good idea to have the project budget reviewed by a financial expert or someone with experience in grant writing. This can help ensure that the budget is comprehensive, realistic, and meets funder expectations.

In addition, having a second set of eyes review the budget can help identify any errors or inconsistencies that may have been overlooked. This can increase the likelihood of securing the grant and ensure that the project is adequately funded.

CASE STUDY

Let's take a closer look at a sample grant proposal for the hypothetical nonprofit introduced in Chapter 1. The nonprofit is called "Green City," and its mission is to promote environmental sustainability in urban areas. Green City hopes to secure funding for a new project focused on increasing access to fresh produce for low-income residents in urban areas.

Below is an annotated sample grant proposal that highlights effective narrative strategies and how Green City addresses the funder's guidelines and expectations.

I. Executive Summary

The executive summary is an overview of the proposal, highlighting the key elements of the project and why it is important. Green City's executive summary should be brief, compelling, and well-written to capture the funder's attention. It should include:

- A brief introduction to Green City and its mission
- A statement of the project's goals and objectives
- An explanation of why the project is important
- A summary of the funding request

II. Problem Statement

The introduction should provide background information on the issue the project is addressing and why it is important. Green City should use this section to:

- Provide context for the project by describing the issue of food insecurity in urban areas
- Explain why this issue is important and the impact it has on the health and well-being of low-income residents
- Describe the challenges and barriers that prevent low-income residents from accessing fresh produce

III. Project Description

This section should provide a detailed description of the project, including its goals, objectives, and methods. Green City should use this section to:

- Clearly state the project's goals and objectives, and explain how they will address the issue of food insecurity
- Provide a timeline for the project, including key milestones and deadlines
- Describe the activities and strategies that will be used to achieve the project's goals
- Explain how the project will be evaluated and measured for success

IV. Organizational Capacity

This section should describe Green City's capacity to carry out the proposed project, including its experience, expertise, and resources. Green City should use this section to:

- Provide information on the organization's history, including past projects and successes
- Describe the staff and volunteer team involved in the project, highlighting their relevant experience and qualifications
- Explain how Green City will use the grant funds to support the project
- Describe any partnerships or collaborations that will support the project

V. Budget and Budget Justification

This section should provide a detailed budget for the project and explain how the funds will be used. Green City should use this section to:

- Provide a detailed budget for the project, including all anticipated expenses and income
- Explain how the budget aligns with the project's goals and objectives

- Provide a budget justification for each line item, explaining why each expense is necessary for the project

VI. Conclusion

The conclusion should reiterate the importance of the project and why Green City is the best organization to carry out the work. Green City should use this section to:

- Thank the funder for considering the proposal
- Restate the project's goals and objectives, and explain how they align with the funder's priorities
- Reinforce Green City's capacity to successfully carry out the project

Overall, the grant proposal for Green City follows a clear and effective narrative structure. The proposal presents a compelling case for the importance of the project, and is well-organized and easy to follow.

The budget is detailed and realistic, and the goals and objectives are well-aligned with the funder's priorities.

By following these guidelines, Green City has created a strong proposal that is likely to be successful in securing funding for their important work.

Chapter 5
Creating Effective Supporting Materials

Once you have crafted a compelling narrative for your grant proposal and have a detailed project plan and budget, it is time to think about creating effective supporting materials. Supporting materials can include a variety of items, such as letters of support, organizational charts, resumes, and marketing materials. These materials can help to reinforce your narrative and provide additional evidence of your nonprofit's ability to carry out the proposed project.

Here are some tips for creating effective supporting materials for your grant proposal:

1. **Letters of Support**: It is often helpful to obtain letters of support from individuals or organizations who are familiar with your nonprofit's work and can attest to the importance and potential impact of your proposed project. When soliciting letters of support, be sure to provide a clear and concise explanation of your project and its goals, as well as any specific information that the letter writer should include, such as the writer's connection to your nonprofit or the project's potential impact on the community. Letters of support should be written on official letterhead and signed by the letter writer.

2. **Organizational Charts**: If your nonprofit is large or has a complex structure, it can be helpful to provide an organizational chart that illustrates the key players involved in the proposed project. This can help funders understand the roles and responsibilities of different staff members and how the project will be managed.

3. **Resumes**: Including resumes of key staff members involved in the proposed project can provide funders with a clear understanding of the experience and expertise of your team. Resumes should highlight relevant work experience and qualifications, as well as any education or training that is directly related to the proposed project.
4. **Marketing Materials**: If your nonprofit has brochures, flyers, or other marketing materials that promote your organization and its programs, consider including these in your grant proposal. These materials can help funders understand the scope and impact of your nonprofit's work, as well as its history of success and community support.
5. **Evaluation Plans**: It is important to include an evaluation plan in your grant proposal that outlines how you will measure the success of your proposed project. This plan should include specific metrics for success, as well as the methods you will use to collect and analyze data. Including an evaluation plan in your grant proposal can demonstrate your nonprofit's commitment to accountability and transparency.
6. **Organizational Brochure**: One key piece of supporting material is an organizational brochure. This should be a professionally-designed document that provides an overview of your nonprofit's mission, history, and key programs. A well-crafted brochure can serve as an excellent leave-behind for funders who want to learn more about your nonprofit after a site visit or meeting.
7. **Case Studies**: Another effective way to demonstrate the impact of your nonprofit is through case studies. These stories should highlight specific individuals or communities that have been positively impacted by your organization's work. A

well-written case study should include the individual's background, the challenges they faced, and the specific ways your nonprofit was able to help them overcome those challenges.

8. **Photos and Videos**: Visual elements such as photos and videos can be a highly effective way to convey your nonprofit's mission and impact. Consider including photos of the individuals or communities you serve, as well as photos that highlight the specific programs or initiatives your nonprofit offers. Videos can be especially impactful, as they allow funders to see and hear directly from the individuals whose lives have been positively impacted by your nonprofit's work.

9. **Financial Statements**: While not the most exciting supporting material, financial statements are a crucial element of any grant proposal. These documents should clearly demonstrate your nonprofit's financial stability and sound management practices. Be sure to include both your organization's most recent audited financial statements and your current year budget.

When creating supporting materials for your grant proposal, it's important to keep in mind the funder's priorities and requirements. Make sure the materials you include are directly relevant to the specific grant you are applying for and are tailored to address the funder's particular areas of interest.

Additionally, it's important to ensure that all of your supporting materials are professionally designed and presented. Poorly designed materials or materials that are difficult to read or understand can detract from the overall strength of your grant proposal. Consider working with a graphic designer or other professional to help you create high-quality materials that effectively convey your nonprofit's message and impact.

In conclusion, supporting materials can play a critical role in a successful grant proposal. By including a range of materials that demonstrate your nonprofit's impact, credibility, and financial stability, you can make a compelling case for why your organization is worthy of funding. Remember to carefully tailor your supporting materials to the specific grant you are applying for, and to present them in a professional and effective manner.

Developing a logic model

Developing a logic model is an important step in the grant writing process. A logic model is a visual representation of the relationships between the resources, activities, outputs, and outcomes of a project. It helps to clarify the purpose of the project and the steps required to achieve success. A logic model is an essential tool for communicating with funders, stakeholders, and staff about the project's goals and objectives.

There are several components to a logic model, including the problem statement, inputs, activities, outputs, outcomes, and impact.

The problem statement is a brief description of the problem or need that the project is designed to address. Inputs are the resources needed to carry out the project, such as staff time, equipment, and supplies.

Activities are the steps that will be taken to address the problem or need, and outputs are the products or services that result from these activities.

Outcomes are the expected changes that will occur as a result of the project. There are two types of outcomes: short-term and long-term. Short-term outcomes are the immediate changes that occur as a result of the project, such as increased knowledge or improved skills. Long-term outcomes are the more significant changes that occur over time, such as improved health outcomes or increased community involvement.

Impact is the ultimate goal of the project and refers to the overall effect of the project on the community or target population. The impact is the highest level of change that the project aims to achieve.

Developing a logic model involves a collaborative process with all stakeholders involved in the project. It is important to identify the resources and activities needed to achieve the desired outcomes and impact. The logic model should be specific, measurable, achievable, relevant, and time-bound (SMART). This means that the goals and objectives of the project should be clear, measurable, and achievable within a specific time frame.

A logic model can be developed using a variety of methods, including brainstorming, focus groups, and surveys. The goal is to create a clear and concise visual representation of the project that communicates the goals and objectives to all stakeholders.

In conclusion, developing a logic model is an essential step in the grant writing process. It helps to clarify the purpose of the project and the steps required to achieve success. A logic model is an essential tool for communicating with funders, stakeholders, and staff about the project's goals and objectives. By following the SMART guidelines and involving all stakeholders in the process, a logic model can be an effective tool for achieving success in a project.

Creating a Project Timeline

Creating a project timeline is a crucial step in the grant proposal writing process. A project timeline is a detailed plan that outlines the various tasks and activities that need to be completed to successfully implement a project.

It provides a clear roadmap for the project team, helps to identify potential bottlenecks and delays, and ensures that the project stays on track and is completed on time.

Here are some tips for creating an effective project timeline:

1. **Start with the end goal in mind:** The first step in creating a project timeline is to identify the end goal or deliverables of the project. These could be specific outcomes, reports, or events that the project is designed to achieve. Once you have identified the end goal, work backward to identify the various tasks that need to be completed to achieve that goal.
2. **Break down the project into smaller tasks:** Once you have identified the various tasks that need to be completed, break them down into smaller, more manageable tasks. This will help to ensure that each task is achievable and that the project team is not overwhelmed by the scope of the project.
3. **Assign deadlines to each task**: Once you have broken down the project into smaller tasks, assign specific

deadlines to each task. These deadlines should be realistic and take into account the time and resources that are available to complete the task.

4. **Identify dependencies between tasks**: Some tasks may be dependent on the completion of others. For example, you may need to complete a survey before you can analyze the results. Identify these dependencies and build them into the project timeline.
5. **Prioritize tasks**: Some tasks may be more critical than others. Prioritize tasks based on their importance to the overall success of the project.
6. **Review and revise**: Once you have created the initial project timeline, review it with the project team and make any necessary revisions. Be open to feedback and suggestions for improvement.
7. **Monitor progress:** Once the project is underway, monitor progress against the project timeline. Identify any delays or potential bottlenecks and take action to address them.

A well-designed project timeline can help to keep your team on track, ensure that tasks are completed on time, and ultimately lead to the successful implementation of your project.

Developing an Evaluation Plan

An evaluation plan is an essential component of any grant proposal. It outlines how a nonprofit organization intends to assess the success of its program or project. Developing an evaluation plan ensures that the organization is held accountable for the grant funds received and that the program is effective in achieving its goals.

Here are some key steps to developing an effective evaluation plan:

1. **Define your evaluation questions:** Evaluation questions are specific inquiries you want to answer about your program. These questions should be developed based on the program goals and objectives. Some examples of evaluation questions could be: Did the program achieve its intended outcomes? Were the program's activities implemented as planned? Did the program meet the needs of the target population?
2. **Determine your evaluation methods**: Evaluation methods are the tools or techniques used to collect data to answer your evaluation questions. Some common evaluation methods include surveys, focus groups, interviews, and observation. It's essential to select methods that will provide the most accurate and reliable data.
3. **Develop your data collection plan:** Your data collection plan outlines the details of how you will collect your data, such as who will collect the data, when, and from whom. It's essential to ensure that your data collection plan is realistic, feasible, and aligned with your evaluation questions.
4. **Identify your data analysis methods:** Once you've collected your data, you need to determine how you will analyze it. This could involve statistical analysis or a more qualitative approach, depending on the evaluation questions and data collected.
5. **Develop a reporting plan:** A reporting plan outlines how you will share your evaluation findings with key stakeholders. This could include a report, a presentation, or other communication methods. It's important to ensure that your reporting plan aligns with the expectations of the grant funder and other stakeholders.

CASE STUDY

Let's consider the hypothetical nonprofit organization, "Community Health Solutions," that aims to improve health outcomes for underserved communities by providing access to healthcare services and educational resources. To achieve their mission, they secured a grant from a local healthcare foundation to implement a community health outreach program.

As part of the grant proposal, Community Health Solutions developed a logic model and an evaluation plan to guide the project's implementation and assess its effectiveness.

Developing a Logic Model:

A logic model is a visual representation that outlines the organization's overall goals, planned activities, and expected outcomes. It helps to create a clear and consistent understanding of how the project will work and how the objectives will be achieved. The components of a logic model include inputs, activities, outputs, and outcomes.

Community Health Solutions' logic model looks like this:

Inputs:

- Funding from the healthcare foundation
- Healthcare providers and staff
- Educational materials on health and wellness
- Partnerships with community organizations

Activities:

- Conduct community health needs assessment to identify the target population's health needs
- Develop and implement an educational curriculum on healthy living
- Conduct health fairs and screenings
- Provide referrals to health care providers and follow-up care
- Monitor and evaluate the project's effectiveness

Outputs:

- Number of people who participated in health fairs and screenings
- Number of referrals made to health care providers
- Number of educational materials distributed

Outcomes:

- Increased awareness and knowledge of health and wellness
- Improved health outcomes for the target population
- Increased access to health care services

By developing a logic model, Community Health Solutions was able to outline a clear and concise understanding of how their program would operate, what would be required to achieve their goals, and how they could measure their success.

Developing an Evaluation Plan:

An evaluation plan outlines how the project's effectiveness will be measured and what indicators will be used to assess progress towards the desired outcomes. The evaluation plan should be aligned with the logic model and the funder's expectations. The components of an evaluation plan include a description of the evaluation design, data collection methods, and analysis and reporting of results.

Community Health Solutions' evaluation plan for their community health outreach program looks like this:

Evaluation Design:

- Quasi-experimental design with pre- and post-intervention measures
- Comparison group for data analysis
- Qualitative data collected from focus groups and key informant interviews

Data Collection Methods:

- Pre- and post-intervention surveys to measure knowledge and awareness of health and wellness
- Health outcome data from electronic health records
- Referral data from healthcare providers
- Focus groups and key informant interviews with program participants and partners

Analysis and Reporting of Results:

- Descriptive statistics to summarize survey and outcome data
- Regression analysis to identify relationships between program participation and health outcomes
- Qualitative analysis of focus groups and key informant interviews
- Regular reports to the funder and the organization's stakeholders

By developing an evaluation plan, Community Health Solutions was able to set measurable objectives that aligned with their logic model and the funder's expectations. They could assess the effectiveness of the program, identify areas for improvement, and demonstrate the program's impact to their stakeholders.

Chapter 6:
Submitting the Grant Proposal

After weeks or even months of hard work, it is finally time to submit your grant proposal. But before you hit that "submit" button, there are a few things you need to keep in mind to ensure your submission is as strong as possible. In this chapter, we'll go over the final steps in the grant writing process, from reviewing and editing your proposal to submitting it to the funder.

1. **Review and Edit Your Proposal**: Before submitting your grant proposal, it's crucial to review and edit it thoroughly. This means checking for spelling and grammar errors, ensuring that your narrative is clear and concise, and making sure that your proposal meets all of the funder's guidelines and requirements.

One effective way to review your proposal is to have someone else read it. Choose a colleague or mentor with experience in grant writing to provide feedback. They can offer valuable insights and help identify any areas that need improvement.

When editing your proposal, pay particular attention to the following:

- **Narrative**: Your narrative should tell a compelling story about your organization and project, and clearly articulate your goals and objectives.
- Budget: Make sure your budget is realistic, and that all expenses are clearly justified.

- **Evaluation plan**: Ensure that your evaluation plan is thorough and will allow you to measure your project's impact over time.
- **Supporting materials**: Double-check that all of your supporting materials, such as your logic model and project timeline, are accurate and clearly presented.
2. **Gather Required Documentation**: Most funders will require some additional documentation to be submitted alongside your grant proposal. This may include your organization's tax-exempt status, financial statements, and a list of board members.

   Make sure you have all of these documents ready to go before submitting your proposal. This will help to streamline the submission process and ensure that your proposal is considered in a timely manner.

3. **Submit Your Proposal:** Once you've reviewed and edited your proposal and gathered all required documentation, it's time to submit your proposal to the funder.

   Each funder will have its own submission process, so make sure you carefully follow their instructions. Some funders will require you to submit your proposal via an online portal, while others may prefer a paper submission.

   When submitting your proposal, be sure to:

- Double-check that all required documents are included
- Submit your proposal before the deadline
- Follow up with the funder to confirm receipt of your proposal
4. **Track Your Proposal's Status**: After submitting your proposal, it's important to keep track of its status. This can help you to prepare for any potential outcomes, and ensure

that you are ready to move forward with your project once you receive a decision.

Some funders will provide regular updates on the status of your proposal, while others may not communicate until a decision has been made. If you haven't heard back from the funder within the expected time frame, it's okay to follow up and ask about the status of your proposal.

5. **Prepare for Potential Outcomes**: Once a decision has been made on your grant proposal, it's important to be prepared for all possible outcomes. If your proposal is accepted, you will need to be ready to move forward with your project and meet all of the funder's requirements.

If your proposal is declined, it's important to take the time to reflect on the feedback provided and identify areas for improvement. This can help you to strengthen your proposal and increase your chances of success in future grant applications.

In conclusion, submitting a grant proposal can be a daunting process, but with careful planning and attention to detail, you can increase your chances of success. By thoroughly reviewing and editing your proposal, gathering all required documentation, following the funder's submission process, tracking your proposal's status, and preparing for potential outcomes,

Understanding the Submission Process

Submitting a grant proposal is the final step in the grant-seeking process. It's important to understand the submission process and all the associated requirements to ensure that your proposal has the best possible chance of being accepted.

Here, we will discuss some important considerations when submitting a grant proposal.

The first step in the submission process is to make sure you have thoroughly reviewed the funder's guidelines and requirements. This will help you ensure that your proposal meets all the necessary criteria, including formatting, word count, and any additional supporting materials. It's important to double-check all of the details to avoid disqualification due to small oversights.

It's also important to ensure that you submit your proposal by the stated deadline. Late submissions are almost never accepted, and it's better to submit early to avoid any last-minute technical issues. In addition, make sure you know the submission method, whether it's through an online portal or by mail, and whether you need to submit any hard copies or additional materials.

Before submitting, it's a good idea to have someone else review your proposal for errors, typos, and clarity. This could be a colleague or a professional grant writer. Having another set of eyes can help catch mistakes and ensure that your proposal is as clear and effective as possible.

Finally, make sure that you have all the necessary supporting documents and information included with your proposal. This could include letters of support from community leaders, a detailed project budget, or other materials specific to the funder's requirements. If you are uncertain about what materials to include, reach out to the funder and ask for clarification.

It's important to remember that the submission process is not the end of the grant-seeking process. Once your proposal has been submitted, it's time to follow up with the funder to ensure that they have received your proposal and to address any questions or concerns they may have. If your proposal is accepted, be sure to express your gratitude and follow through with your proposed project plan and evaluation plan. If your proposal is declined, reach out to the funder and ask for feedback to improve your proposal for future grant-seeking opportunities.

In summary, submitting a grant proposal requires careful attention to detail and adherence to the funder's guidelines and requirements. By understanding the submission process and taking the necessary steps to ensure that your proposal is thorough and well-written, you can increase your chances of success in securing grant funding for your nonprofit organization.

Ensuring Compliance with all Requirements

When submitting a grant proposal, it's essential to make sure that you comply with all the requirements set by the funder. Failure to comply with the guidelines can result in your proposal being rejected, even if it is otherwise excellent.

Here are some tips to help you ensure compliance with all requirements:

1. **Read the guidelines thoroughly**: Before you start writing your grant proposal, make sure to read the guidelines provided by the funder. Read them thoroughly and take note of all the requirements that you need to comply with.

2. **Follow the guidelines strictly**: Once you've read the guidelines, make sure to follow them strictly. If the funder has specific formatting requirements, make sure to follow them. If they require a certain number of copies, make sure to provide that exact number.
3. **Submit all required documents:** Some funders may require additional documents along with your grant proposal, such as financial statements or proof of nonprofit status. Make sure to submit all the required documents.
4. **Proofread your proposal**: Before submitting your proposal, make sure to proofread it thoroughly. Check for typos, grammatical errors, and other mistakes that may make your proposal look unprofessional.
5. **Submit on time**: Make sure to submit your grant proposal on time. Most funders have strict deadlines, and late submissions are often not accepted.
6. **Track your submission**: After you've submitted your proposal, keep track of its status. Make note of the date you submitted it, the name of the person you submitted it to, and any other important information. This can help you follow up if you don't hear back from the funder within the expected timeframe.

Preparing for Follow up Communication with the Funder

After submitting a grant proposal, it's important to remember that the process is not over yet. Follow-up communication with the funder can be a critical component of the grant application process, as it can help clarify any misunderstandings and give the nonprofit an opportunity to make their case in person or on the phone. In this section, we'll explore how to prepare for follow-up communication with the funder.

1. **Review your proposal**: Before you begin preparing for follow-up communication, take the time to review your

proposal. This will help you refresh your memory on the details of the project and the specific requests made by the funder. Be sure to review your budget, timeline, and supporting materials to ensure that you have a solid understanding of the proposal as a whole.

2. **Develop a list of potential questions**: As you review your proposal, develop a list of potential questions that the funder may ask. Consider any potential areas of confusion, as well as any questions that the funder may have about the project, the budget, or the organization itself. This can help you prepare for follow-up communication and ensure that you have a solid understanding of the project and the expectations of the funder.

3. **Be prepared to answer questions about your organization**: In addition to questions about the project itself, funders may also have questions about your organization as a whole. Be prepared to discuss your organization's mission, history, and track record of success. It's also a good idea to have information on hand about your team members and their qualifications, as well as any partnerships or collaborations that may be relevant to the project.

4. **Be open to feedback**: Follow-up communication with a funder can also be an opportunity to receive feedback on your proposal. Be open to constructive criticism and be prepared to address any concerns that the funder may have. This can help you refine your proposal and make it more compelling to future funders.

5. **Follow up in a timely manner**: If a funder requests additional information or follow-up communication, be sure to respond in a timely manner. This demonstrates your commitment to the project and your respect for the funder's time and resources. If you need additional time to gather information or respond to questions, be sure to communicate this clearly and promptly.

6. **Be professional and respectful**: Finally, it's important to remember that follow-up communication is an opportunity to build a relationship with the funder. Be professional and respectful in all of your communications, and demonstrate a genuine interest in the funder's priorities and goals. This can help you establish a positive relationship that may be beneficial for future grant opportunities.

Preparing for follow-up communication with a funder is an important component of the grant application process. By reviewing your proposal, developing a list of potential questions, being prepared to answer questions about your organization, being open to feedback, following up in a timely manner, and being professional and respectful in all communications, you can maximize your chances of success and build a positive relationship with the funder.

CASE STUDY

Submitting a grant proposal can be an arduous process, but it can also be very rewarding if done correctly.

In order to be successful, it is important to have a solid understanding of the submission process, including how to ensure compliance with all requirements and how to prepare for follow-up communication with the funder.

To provide a practical example, let's walk through the submission process for a specific grant opportunity and examine how a nonprofit can ensure compliance and address potential challenges.

Our hypothetical nonprofit, Community Gardens, has identified a grant opportunity that aligns with their mission to provide healthy food options for under-resourced communities. The grant requires a detailed project proposal and a clear plan for measuring impact.

Step 1: Read and Understand the Guidelines

The first step in the submission process is to carefully read and understand the grant guidelines. This may seem like a no-brainer, but it is a critical step that should not be overlooked. Pay close attention to the eligibility criteria, funding priorities, and any specific requirements or restrictions outlined in the guidelines.

Community Gardens finds that the grant requires a 10-page proposal and a project budget, along with a detailed plan for evaluating the project's impact. They also note that the grant prioritizes projects that focus on sustainability and equitable distribution of resources.

Step 2: Develop a Project Proposal and Budget

Next, Community Gardens begins developing their project proposal and budget, taking care to align their goals with the grant priorities and guidelines. They conduct research and gather data to support their proposal, and ensure that their budget is realistic and detailed.

Community Gardens also decides to incorporate a logic model and evaluation plan into their proposal, in order to clearly demonstrate how their project aligns with the grant priorities and how they plan to measure their impact over time.

Step 3: Review and Edit

Once the proposal and budget are complete, it is important to thoroughly review and edit them to ensure that they meet all the grant requirements and are free of errors. This includes ensuring that the proposal is within the required page limit, that all necessary sections are included, and that the budget is clear and accurate.

Community Gardens also takes care to ensure that their logic model and evaluation plan are well-organized and easy to understand, and that they clearly articulate how their project will achieve the desired outcomes and measure its impact.

Step 4: Submit the Proposal

Finally, it is time to submit the proposal. Community Gardens carefully follows the submission instructions outlined in the grant guidelines, including formatting requirements, file type, and deadline.

After the proposal is submitted, Community Gardens follows up with the funder to confirm receipt and thank them for the opportunity to apply. They also prepare for potential follow-up communication by designating a point of contact and ensuring that they have the necessary resources and data available.

Chapter 7
Post submission, what happens next?

Congratulations! You've submitted your grant proposal. Now what?

What happens after you hit that "submit" button? This can be a nerve-wracking time for nonprofits as you wait to hear back from the funder.

But there are steps you can take to increase your chances of success and prepare for the next steps in the process.

First, it's important to remember that the timeline for hearing back from a funder can vary widely depending on the funder and the type of grant. Some funders may respond within a few weeks, while others may take several months.

Before submitting your grant proposal, make sure you have a good understanding of the timeline so you can plan accordingly.

One of the first steps you should take after submitting your grant proposal is to follow up with the funder.

This can help ensure that they received your proposal and can also provide an opportunity for you to ask any questions you may have about the review process. Some funders may also provide feedback on your proposal, which can be valuable information for future grant applications.

During this time, it's also important to keep track of any communications you have with the funder. Make note of any questions or concerns they may have, and be sure to respond in a timely and professional manner.

As you wait for a response from the funder, you can also take steps to prepare for the next steps in the process. If your proposal is approved, you'll need to be ready to start implementing your project. This may involve setting up new programs or services, hiring staff, or purchasing equipment or supplies. Make sure you have a plan in place to handle these tasks if your proposal is approved.

You should also be prepared to provide regular updates to the funder on the progress of your project. This may involve submitting progress reports, financial reports, and other documentation as required by the funder. Make sure you understand the reporting requirements for your grant and are prepared to meet them.

If your proposal is not approved, don't be discouraged. Use the feedback provided by the funder to improve your proposal and try again in the future. You can also reach out to the funder to ask for feedback on why your proposal was not accepted. This can help you identify areas for improvement and increase your chances of success in the future.

The post-submission phase of the grant process is a critical time for nonprofits. It's important to stay engaged with the funder and be prepared for the next steps in the process.

By following up with the funder, preparing for project implementation, and being ready to provide regular updates, you can increase your chances of success and maximize the impact of your grant-funded project.

Understanding the Grant Review Process

Once you submit your grant proposal, the review process begins. Understanding the grant review process is essential for nonprofits seeking funding, as it can help them understand how their proposal will be evaluated and what they can expect in terms of feedback.

The grant review process can vary depending on the funder and the type of grant being reviewed.

However, most grant review processes involve the following steps:

1. **Initial screening**: The grant application is initially screened to ensure it meets the funder's eligibility criteria, and that all required documents and forms are included.
2. **Peer review:** The grant application is assigned to a peer review panel made up of experts in the relevant field. The panel evaluates the proposal based on the funder's selection criteria.
3. **Reviewer feedback**: After reviewing the proposal, the peer review panel provides feedback to the funder. This feedback may be in the form of written comments, scores or rankings.
4. **Final decision**: Based on the feedback from the peer review panel, the funder makes a final decision on whether to award the grant.

It is important to note that the review process can take several months, and nonprofits may not receive feedback until after the funding decision has been made.

To ensure that your proposal is competitive, it is important to carefully review the funder's selection criteria and tailor your proposal to meet their expectations. This includes demonstrating a clear understanding of the problem you are addressing, providing a detailed plan for achieving your goals, and demonstrating your organization's capacity to successfully implement the project.

It is also important to ensure that your proposal is well-written, clear, and easy to follow. Consider asking colleagues or partners to review your proposal before submitting it to ensure that it is compelling, error-free, and well-organized.

During the review process, it is important to be patient and proactive. Keep in mind that funders may receive hundreds or even thousands of applications, and it may take some time to receive feedback. You may want to follow up with the funder after a few weeks or months to inquire about the status of your proposal.

If your proposal is rejected, it is important to view this as an opportunity to learn and improve. Review the feedback provided by the peer review panel and use it to refine your proposal for future grant opportunities.

In some cases, your proposal may be selected for funding but for a lower amount than requested. If this happens, consider revising your project budget and timeline to ensure that the project can still be successfully implemented with the reduced funding.

Overall, the grant review process can be lengthy and challenging, but understanding the process and following best practices can increase your chances of success.

Preparing for the Site Visits or Interviews

After submitting a grant proposal, your nonprofit may be asked to participate in a site visit or interview as part of the grant review process. This is an important opportunity to showcase your organization and demonstrate how your proposed project aligns with the funder's priorities.

Preparing for a site visit or interview can be a daunting task, but with careful planning and attention to detail, you can ensure that you make the most of this opportunity. Here are some key steps to help you prepare:

1. **Review the funder's guidelines and expectations.** As with any aspect of the grant process, it's important to carefully review the funder's guidelines and expectations for site visits or interviews. This may include details on who will be conducting the visit or interview, what topics will be covered, and what materials or documentation you should have prepared. Make sure you have a clear understanding of what is expected of you so that you can prepare accordingly.
2. **Gather the necessary materials**. Depending on the funder's requirements, you may need to provide additional documentation or materials to support your proposal during the site visit or interview. This could include financial statements, progress reports, or examples of previous work your organization has done. Be sure to gather these materials well in advance so that you have time to review and organize them.
3. **Identify key messages and talking points**. The site visit or interview is an opportunity for you to showcase your organization and your proposed project. Identify the key messages and talking points you want to convey, and make sure that all staff and volunteers who will be participating in the visit or interview are aware of them. This will ensure

that everyone is on the same page and that your message is consistent.

4. **Prepare your team**. If multiple staff and volunteers will be participating in the site visit or interview, make sure that everyone is well prepared. This may include providing training or guidance on how to present your organization and your proposed project in the best possible light. Encourage team members to practice their talking points and anticipate potential questions or challenges that may arise.

5. **Be organized and professional**. During the site visit or interview, it's important to be organized and professional. Make sure that all necessary materials are readily available and that you are prepared to answer questions or provide additional information as needed. Dress appropriately and maintain a positive attitude throughout the visit or interview.

6. **Follow up**. After the site visit or interview, make sure to follow up with the funder to thank them for their time and provide any additional information or materials that may have been requested. This is also an opportunity to ask any questions you may have about the review process or the status of your grant proposal.

Preparing for a site visit or interview as part of the grant review process requires careful planning, attention to detail, and a strong commitment to presenting your organization and your proposed project in the best possible light.

By following these key steps, you can ensure that you are well prepared and that you make the most of this important opportunity.

Evaluating and Responding to Feedback

When it comes to the grant application process, feedback can be incredibly valuable. It can help you improve your proposal, better understand the funder's priorities, and ultimately increase your chances of securing funding. That said, receiving feedback can be challenging, especially if it's critical or if you feel strongly about the direction of your project. In this article, we'll provide some tips for effectively evaluating and responding to feedback on your grant proposal.

1. **Keep an open mind**: It's important to approach feedback with an open mind. Try to put your personal feelings aside and consider the feedback objectively. Remember that the person giving you feedback is likely trying to help you improve your proposal, not tear it down.
2. **Take notes As you receive feedback, take detailed notes.** Write down both positive and negative comments, as well as any specific suggestions for improvement. This will help you keep track of the feedback and ensure that you don't forget any important points.
3. **Look for patterns**: As you review your notes, look for patterns in the feedback you received. If multiple people gave you the same feedback, it's likely that this is an area that needs improvement.
4. **Consider the source of the feedback**. Is it coming from someone who has expertise in your field? Or is it from someone who is less familiar with your project? While all feedback can be valuable, it's important to take into account the experience and knowledge of the person giving the feedback.
5. **Be grateful**: Remember to express gratitude to those who provided feedback. Even if you don't agree with all of the comments, it's important to thank the person for taking the time to review your proposal and provide input.

6. **Respond thoughtfully**: When responding to feedback, take the time to craft a thoughtful response. Address each point that was raised and explain how you plan to address any concerns or make improvements. If you don't plan to make a specific change, explain why.

7. **Don't be defensive**: It can be tempting to get defensive when receiving feedback, especially if you feel strongly about your proposal. However, it's important to stay open to the feedback and avoid becoming defensive. Remember that the person giving you feedback is trying to help you improve your proposal, not attack it.

8. **Use the feedback to improve your proposal**: Finally, use the feedback to make improvements to your proposal. Take the suggestions that were made and use them to strengthen your proposal. Remember, the goal is to create the best possible proposal, and feedback can help you achieve that goal.

CASE STUDY

Let's dive into a practical example of a nonprofit that received a grant and how they managed it effectively over time.

The nonprofit organization, "Health for All," is dedicated to improving access to healthcare for underserved populations in developing countries. In 2018, Health for All submitted a grant proposal to a major international foundation and was awarded a grant of $500,000 to fund a two-year project in Tanzania.

After receiving the grant, Health for All's project team immediately began preparing for the implementation phase. They knew that the foundation would conduct site visits and interviews to monitor their progress and ensure that the funds were being used appropriately. To prepare for this, they developed a detailed plan for managing the project and engaging with the foundation throughout the process.

One of the first steps Health for All took was to create a project timeline with key milestones and deadlines. They also developed a comprehensive budget that broke down the costs for each aspect of the project. These tools helped the team stay on track and track their progress, as well as provide a clear picture of how the grant funds were being used.

To address feedback from the foundation, Health for All worked closely with the foundation to establish clear communication channels and expectations for site visits and reporting. They assigned specific team members to be responsible for different aspects of the project and to act as liaisons with the foundation.

In addition, Health for All recognized the importance of continuous evaluation and feedback throughout the project. They set up regular check-ins with their local partners in Tanzania to assess the impact of the project and make any necessary adjustments to their plans. They also conducted surveys and focus groups to gather feedback from the community, and incorporated that feedback into their project planning and implementation.

Overall, Health for All's proactive approach to project management and their commitment to open communication and continuous evaluation played a critical role in the success of their project. They were able to address any concerns or challenges that arose, and used the feedback *they received to improve their approach and make a greater impact in the community.*

When the grant period ended, Health for All was able to demonstrate to the foundation that they had used the funds effectively and made a significant impact on the health outcomes of the community they served. As a result, the foundation offered them continued support and resources to further their mission.

In conclusion, effectively managing a grant-funded project requires careful planning, communication, and evaluation. By using tools like project timelines, detailed budgets, and logic models, nonprofits can stay on track and measure their impact over time. Establishing clear communication channels with funders and local partners is also crucial for addressing feedback and concerns that arise during the project. With a proactive and responsive approach, nonprofits can successfully manage their grant funds and make a significant impact in the communities they serve.

Chapter 8
Stewarding the grant

Congratulations! You've received a grant, and now you're tasked with stewarding the grant funds and ensuring the project stays on track. This is where the real work begins. In this chapter, we'll explore the key components of stewarding a grant and how to manage the grant funds effectively.

1. **Understanding the Grant Agreement**: Before you can start stewarding the grant funds, it's important to thoroughly review the grant agreement. The grant agreement outlines the terms and conditions of the grant, including the scope of the project, the budget, and the timeline. It's essential to ensure that your organization is in compliance with all of the requirements and restrictions outlined in the grant agreement.

2. **Establishing a System for Grant Management**: Effective grant management requires a clear and organized system to keep track of the grant funds and ensure that they are being used for their intended purpose. This system should include a budget plan, a record-keeping process, and regular check-ins to ensure that the project is meeting its goals.

3. **Establishing a Communication Plan with the Funder**: It's important to establish a communication plan with the funder to ensure that they are kept informed of the project's progress and any challenges that arise. This communication plan should include regular updates and reports on the project's progress, as well as opportunities for feedback and input from the funder.

4. **Tracking and Reporting Grant Expenditures**: To effectively steward the grant funds, it's important to track

and report all expenditures associated with the project. This includes not only tracking the expenses themselves but also maintaining documentation such as receipts and invoices. The grant agreement may also require regular financial reports to be submitted to the funder.

5. **Monitoring and Evaluating Project Progress**: To ensure that the project is staying on track and meeting its goals, it's important to regularly monitor and evaluate its progress. This can include tracking metrics such as the number of people served, the amount of progress made toward the project's goals, and any challenges that arise. This information should be used to inform any necessary course corrections or adjustments to the project.

6. **Managing Grant Closeout**: When the grant period is coming to an end, it's important to effectively manage the closeout process. This may include submitting final reports to the funder, documenting all expenditures associated with the project, and ensuring that any remaining funds are used in accordance with the grant agreement.

Managing Grant's Funds Effectively

Managing grant funds effectively is crucial to the success of any nonprofit project. It is important to understand that grant funds come with specific rules and regulations that must be followed to ensure compliance with the funder's expectations.

Here are some key considerations for managing grant funds effectively:

1. **Set up a system for tracking expenses**: It is essential to set up a tracking system to ensure that all expenses are recorded accurately and can be easily accessed when needed. This will help ensure that funds are used for the

purposes intended by the grant and will allow for accurate reporting to the funder.

2. **Follow the funder's guidelines for reporting**: Grant funds often come with reporting requirements, including specific deadlines and reporting formats. It is crucial to follow these guidelines to ensure that the project remains in good standing with the funder and to avoid any potential issues with future grant opportunities.

3. **Use funds only for the purposes intended by the grant**: It is important to use grant funds only for the purposes outlined in the grant proposal. If changes to the project are necessary, it is important to discuss them with the funder and seek approval before making any changes.

4. **Maintain communication with the funder**: Regular communication with the funder is essential for effective management of grant funds. This includes providing regular updates on the project's progress and any changes that may impact the use of grant funds.

5. **Keep accurate records:** It is essential to keep accurate records of all financial transactions related to the project. This includes receipts, invoices, and other financial documents that may be required for reporting purposes.

6. **Monitor the budget regularly**: Regular monitoring of the budget can help ensure that grant funds are being used effectively and that the project is on track to meet its goals. This will also allow for early identification of any potential issues or challenges.

Communicating with Funders and Stakeholders

When it comes to grant management, one of the most critical aspects is communication. Clear and regular communication with funders and stakeholders can help ensure that the grant-funded project runs smoothly and that everyone involved is on the same page.

Here are some tips on effective communication with funders and stakeholders during grant management:

1. **Establish a Communication Plan**: It's important to establish a clear communication plan at the start of the grant-funded project. This plan should outline how often you will communicate with funders and stakeholders, what information you will provide, and how you will deliver that information. This plan can be included in your grant proposal and agreed upon by all parties involved.

2. **Be Transparent: Transparency is key to effective communication**. Be transparent about the progress of the project, any challenges or roadblocks, and how you are using the grant funds. Funders want to see that their investment is being used effectively and efficiently, and stakeholders want to know that the project is making a positive impact.

3. **Use Multiple Communication Channels**: Different stakeholders may prefer to receive information in different ways. Some may prefer email updates, while others may prefer phone calls or in-person meetings. Use a mix of communication channels to ensure that everyone is receiving the information they need in a way that works for them.

4. **Provide Regular Updates:** Regular updates are crucial to keeping funders and stakeholders informed about the project's progress. Provide updates on a regular basis, whether it's weekly, monthly, or quarterly, and be sure to include key metrics and outcomes that demonstrate the project's impact.

5. **Be Responsive**: If a funder or stakeholder reaches out with a question or concern, it's important to be responsive and address their concerns in a timely manner. This helps build trust and demonstrates your commitment to the project's success.

6. **Celebrate Successes**: Don't forget to celebrate the project's successes along the way. Share milestones and achievements with funders and stakeholders, and show them how their investment is making a difference.

Meeting Grant Reporting Requirements

Meeting grant reporting requirements is an essential component of effectively managing grant funds and fulfilling the expectations of funders. Reporting provides an opportunity for nonprofits to communicate their progress and impact to funders, and to ensure that grant funds are being used in the intended way. In this chapter, we will discuss the importance of meeting grant reporting requirements and provide tips for creating effective reports.

Why Grant Reporting is Important

Grant reporting serves several purposes, including:

1. **Accountability**: Grant reporting demonstrates to funders that nonprofit organizations are using grant funds in the manner for which they were intended.
2. **Communication**: Grant reports enable nonprofits to keep funders updated on their progress and to communicate the impact of their work.
3. **Relationship building**: Effective grant reporting can help build and strengthen relationships with funders, potentially leading to future funding opportunities.
4. **Learning and improvement**: By collecting and analyzing data for grant reports, nonprofits can learn from their experiences and improve their programs and services.

Tips for Effective Grant Reporting

1. **Understand the reporting requirements**: Before accepting a grant, nonprofits should review the reporting requirements and ensure that they are able to meet them. The requirements may include a timeline for reporting, specific metrics to be measured, and the format and content of the report.
2. **Create a reporting plan**: It is important to create a reporting plan that outlines the timeline, metrics, and content of the report. The plan should be reviewed regularly to ensure that the reporting remains on track.
3. **Collect and analyze data**: Nonprofits should collect data on program activities, outputs, and outcomes to demonstrate progress toward the grant objectives. This data should be analyzed to identify successes, challenges, and areas for improvement.
4. **Tell a story:** Grant reports should tell a compelling story of the impact of the nonprofit's work. Use data to demonstrate progress and success, but also include anecdotes and personal stories that illustrate the impact of the program.
5. **Be transparent:** It is important to be transparent in grant reporting. If the program is not meeting the grant objectives or there are challenges, it is important to report this to the funder and provide a plan for addressing the issues.
6. **Use the reporting process as an opportunity for learning and improvement**: Use the reporting process to reflect on program successes and challenges, and identify areas for improvement. Incorporate this learning into the program design and implementation.
7. **Meet reporting deadlines**: Nonprofits should ensure that they meet reporting deadlines to maintain a positive relationship with the funder and demonstrate accountability.

CASE STUDY

Managing grant funds effectively is crucial to the success of any nonprofit organization. It requires careful planning, clear communication with funders and stakeholders, and accurate reporting. In this article, we'll provide a checklist of best practices to help ensure that your nonprofit is effectively managing its grant funds.

1. **Develop a clear plan for using the grant funds**: Before you start spending the grant funds, it's important to have a clear plan in place for how you will use them. This plan should include specific goals and objectives, as well as a timeline for achieving them. Having a clear plan in place will help you stay on track and avoid any potential missteps.
2. **Communicate regularly with your funders**: Regular communication with your funders is essential for building a strong relationship and ensuring that you are meeting their expectations. Be sure to keep them updated on the progress of your project and any challenges that arise. Also, be responsive to any requests for additional information or data.
3. **Monitor your budget and expenses closely**: It's important to keep a close eye on your budget and expenses to ensure that you are staying on track with your project's financial goals. This includes tracking all expenses and comparing them to your budget on a regular basis. If you find that you are running over budget in a particular area, you may need to make adjustments to your spending.
4. **Create accurate reports**: Grant reporting is an essential part of managing grant funds effectively. Be sure to create accurate reports that detail your progress and any challenges that have arisen. Your reports should also include financial information, such as how the grant funds were spent and any remaining funds that are available.

5. **Stay on track with project timelines**: Meeting project timelines is essential for ensuring that you are making progress toward your goals and objectives. Be sure to monitor your timeline closely and make adjustments as needed. If you find that you are falling behind schedule, you may need to make changes to your project plan.

6. **Involve stakeholders in the process**: Involving stakeholders in the grant management process can help ensure that everyone is on the same page and working toward the same goals. This includes communicating regularly with staff, board members, and other stakeholders to keep them updated on your progress.

7. **Seek out additional funding as needed**: If you find that you need additional funding to complete your project, it's important to reach out to your funders as soon as possible. Be prepared to make a strong case for why additional funding is needed and how it will be used.

8. **Build relationships with other funders:** While you may be focused on managing your current grant, it's also important to build relationships with other funders who may be interested in supporting your organization in the future. This includes networking with other nonprofit organizations, attending conferences, and other events where funders may be present.

Chapter 9
Common Grant writing challenges and solutions

Grant writing can be a challenging and complex process. Many nonprofit organizations encounter common grant writing challenges that can impede their ability to secure funding. In this chapter, we will explore these challenges and provide solutions to help overcome them.

Challenge 1: Finding the right funding opportunities

One of the biggest challenges nonprofits face is finding the right funding opportunities. Many organizations are not aware of the different types of funding opportunities available to them or may struggle to identify which opportunities are the best fit for their mission and programs.

Solution: To overcome this challenge, nonprofits should conduct thorough research to identify potential funding opportunities. They should create a list of potential funders and research their eligibility requirements, priorities, and funding priorities. This will help the organization to identify which opportunities are the best fit for their mission and programs.

Challenge 2: Developing a compelling narrative

Another challenge is developing a compelling narrative that effectively conveys the organization's mission, goals, and programs. It can be challenging to create a compelling narrative that captures the funder's attention and conveys the impact of the organization's work.

Solution: To overcome this challenge, nonprofits should focus on storytelling and use concrete examples to demonstrate the impact of their work. They should use data and statistics to support their claims and illustrate the impact of their programs. Additionally, nonprofits should avoid jargon and complex language, and instead, focus on clear and concise language that is accessible to a wide audience.

Challenge 3: Developing a realistic budget

Developing a realistic budget is another common challenge faced by nonprofits. Many organizations struggle to create a budget that accurately reflects the cost of their programs and operations.

Solution: To overcome this challenge, nonprofits should conduct a thorough analysis of their expenses and identify all of the costs associated with their programs and operations. They should also include a line item for unforeseen expenses, such as unexpected program costs or emergencies. Additionally, nonprofits should consider seeking input from financial experts or consultants to ensure that their budget is realistic and accurately reflects their costs.

Challenge 4: Meeting deadlines

Meeting deadlines is crucial to securing funding, but it can be a significant challenge for nonprofits. Many organizations struggle to manage their time effectively and meet grant application and reporting deadlines.

Solution: To overcome this challenge, nonprofits should create a detailed timeline that outlines all grant application and reporting deadlines. They should also assign specific tasks and responsibilities to team members and hold regular check-ins to ensure that everyone is on track. Additionally, nonprofits should consider setting internal deadlines that are earlier than the actual grant deadlines to ensure that they have plenty of time to review and revise their application or report.

Challenge 5: Addressing the funder's expectations

Addressing the funder's expectations can be a challenge for nonprofits. Each funder may have specific requirements, priorities, and expectations for their grantees, which can be challenging for organizations to navigate.

Solution: To overcome this challenge, nonprofits should thoroughly research the funder and their priorities. They should review the funder's website, previous grant awards, and annual reports to gain a better understanding of the funder's goals and expectations. Additionally, nonprofits should consider reaching out to the funder for clarification if they have any questions or concerns about the application or reporting requirements.

In conclusion, grant writing can be challenging, but by addressing these common challenges and implementing best practices, nonprofits can increase their chances of securing funding and effectively managing their grants.

By conducting thorough research, developing a compelling narrative, creating a realistic budget, managing time effectively, and addressing the funder's expectations, nonprofits can overcome these challenges and achieve their goals.

Addressing gaps in experience or capacity

Addressing gaps in experience or capacity is a common challenge for many nonprofits seeking grant funding. Grant funders often look for organizations that have a track record of success in their specific area of focus, which can make it difficult for newer or smaller organizations to compete. However, there are several strategies that nonprofits can use to address these gaps and strengthen their grant proposals.

One effective approach is to form partnerships with other organizations that have complementary skills and expertise. By working with other nonprofits, community groups, or even for-profit businesses, a nonprofit can pool resources and create a stronger, more competitive proposal. For example, if a nonprofit has experience in youth programming but lacks expertise in fundraising, they may partner with a fundraising consultant to strengthen their grant proposal.

Another strategy is to invest in training and capacity building. Many grant funders are willing to support nonprofits that are working to develop their skills and expand their capacity. Nonprofits can seek out training opportunities in areas such as grant writing, program evaluation, and financial management. This not only helps them to build their skills and knowledge, but also demonstrates a commitment to ongoing learning and improvement.

Nonprofits can also address gaps in experience or capacity by focusing on their strengths and unique qualities. Every nonprofit has something to offer that sets them apart from other organizations. By identifying and highlighting these strengths, a nonprofit can make a compelling case for funding. For example, a small grassroots organization may not have a large staff or extensive resources, but they may have deep roots in the community and a unique perspective on the needs of their constituents.

Finally, nonprofits can address gaps in experience or capacity by being transparent and honest about their challenges. Grant funders appreciate honesty and are often willing to work with nonprofits that are upfront about their limitations. By acknowledging their gaps in experience or capacity, nonprofits can demonstrate a willingness to learn and grow, which can make them more appealing to funders.

Overcoming writer's block and procrastination

Writer's block and procrastination are two common challenges that many grant writers face. These issues can lead to missed deadlines, poor quality proposals, and lost opportunities for funding. However, there are several strategies that can help overcome these challenges and improve the grant writing process.

One of the main causes of writer's block and procrastination is a lack of clarity about the project or the grant requirements. Before starting to write the proposal, it is essential to have a clear understanding of the project goals, objectives, and strategies. This can involve conducting research, reviewing past grant proposals, and consulting with stakeholders to gain a better understanding of the project's needs and challenges.

Once you have a clear understanding of the project, it's important to create a detailed outline or roadmap for the proposal. This can help you stay organized and focused on the key points of the proposal, making it easier to write and revise. The outline should include an introduction, project description, needs assessment, goals and objectives, activities and methods, evaluation plan, and budget.

Another effective strategy for overcoming writer's block and procrastination is to set specific and achievable goals for the writing process. This can include setting deadlines for each section of the proposal, such as completing the introduction by a certain date or finishing the evaluation plan by another date. By breaking the writing process into manageable tasks, you can reduce the overwhelm and make steady progress towards the final proposal.

It's also important to create a supportive and productive writing environment. This can involve setting aside dedicated time for writing, finding a quiet and comfortable space to work, and eliminating distractions such as social media or email notifications. It can also be helpful to work with a writing partner or coach, who can provide feedback and support throughout the writing process.

Finally, taking care of yourself and managing stress is essential for maintaining focus and productivity. This can involve practicing self-care activities such as exercise, meditation, or hobbies, and taking breaks when needed to avoid burnout. Additionally, recognizing and managing negative thoughts or emotions that can arise during the writing process can also help to overcome writer's block and procrastination.

Responding to Rejection and Learning from Feedback

Here's the in-depth content on responding to rejection and learning from feedback:

Grant writing can be a long and challenging process, and there is no guarantee that your proposal will be accepted. Despite your best efforts, rejection can be disheartening, but it is an opportunity to learn and grow as a grant writer. Responding to rejection and learning from feedback are critical skills for success in grant writing. In this chapter, we will discuss how to respond to rejection and use feedback to improve your grant writing skills.

Rejection is a part of the grant writing process. It is not uncommon to receive rejections, even after submitting multiple proposals. However, it is essential to respond to rejection in a positive and constructive manner. Here are some tips to help you respond to rejection:

1. **Take time to process your emotions**: Rejection can be discouraging and cause you to doubt your abilities. It is normal to feel upset, disappointed, or frustrated. Take time to acknowledge and process your emotions, but don't let them discourage you from continuing to pursue grant opportunities.
2. **Seek feedback**: After a rejection, you should ask the funder for feedback on your proposal. This will help you understand why your proposal was rejected and provide insights into areas that need improvement. Use this feedback constructively to improve your future proposals.
3. **Review your proposal**: Go back and review your proposal with a critical eye. Look for areas that you can improve or revise. This will help you identify weaknesses and improve your proposal for future submissions.
4. **Consider your options**: After a rejection, it's important to consider your options. You may decide to revise and resubmit the proposal or look for other funding opportunities. Take some time to weigh your options and choose the best path forward.

Learning from feedback is crucial to improving your grant writing skills. Here are some tips to help you learn from feedback:

1. **Listen carefully**: When you receive feedback, listen carefully to what the funder is saying. It is essential to understand the feedback fully and consider it in the context of your proposal.
2. **Keep an open mind:** Be open to suggestions and critiques. Even if you disagree with the feedback, consider the perspectives of the funder and how you can incorporate their feedback into your future proposals.
3. **Look for patterns**: Look for patterns in the feedback you receive. If multiple funders are providing similar feedback, it's a sign that this is an area that needs improvement.
4. **Use the feedback to improve**: Use the feedback you receive to improve your future proposals. If the feedback suggests changes to the project design, budget, or evaluation plan, consider making those changes in your next proposal.

CASE STUDY

Grant writing can be a challenging process, especially for nonprofits that are working with limited resources and staff. However, with the right strategies and mindset, it is possible to overcome common grant writing challenges and secure funding for your organization's mission.

We will explore real-world examples of nonprofits that have faced common grant writing challenges and successfully secured funding by learning from their mistakes and adapting their approach.

Limited Staff Capacity

One common challenge for nonprofits is a limited staff capacity to manage grant writing and other fundraising efforts. This was the case for a small nonprofit in rural Oregon that provided educational programs for underserved youth. With only a part-time staff member to manage grant writing and fundraising, the organization struggled to secure the funding it needed to sustain its programs.

To overcome this challenge, the organization decided to build relationships with local foundations and individual donors. They focused on networking and building personal connections with potential funders, which helped them secure several small grants and individual donations.

Additionally, the organization sought out volunteer grant writers to help manage their grant writing workload. They reached out to local universities and community organizations and were able to find several volunteers with experience in grant writing who were willing to donate their time and skills.

Lack of Experience

Another common challenge for nonprofits is a lack of experience in grant writing. This was the case for a small community center in an urban area that provided after-school programs for low-income youth. Although the center had a strong program track record, its staff had limited experience in grant writing.

To address this challenge, the organization sought out training and resources on grant writing. They attended workshops and conferences on grant writing, and also reached out to other nonprofits in their area for advice and guidance.

The organization also sought out pro-bono or low-cost consulting services to help them develop a strong grant proposal. They connected with a local consulting firm that provided free services to nonprofits, and were able to receive assistance in crafting their proposal and identifying potential funders.

Rejection and Learning from Feedback

Even when nonprofits put in their best efforts, grant applications can be rejected for a variety of reasons. While it can be discouraging to receive a rejection notice, it is important to view it as an opportunity to learn from feedback and improve your approach for future applications.

One example of a nonprofit that faced rejection and used feedback to improve their approach was a small environmental advocacy group that sought funding for a conservation project. Their initial proposal was rejected by a foundation, but the foundation provided detailed feedback on what areas of the proposal needed improvement.

The organization took the feedback seriously and sought out additional resources to improve their proposal. They reached out to other nonprofits in their area for advice and feedback, and also sought out consulting services to help them refine their approach.

After making significant improvements to their proposal, the organization reapplied to the same foundation and was ultimately awarded the grant. They credited their success to their willingness to learn from feedback and make improvements to their approach.

In conclusion, grant writing can be a challenging process for nonprofits, but with the right strategies and mindset, it is possible to overcome common challenges and secure funding for your organization's mission. By building personal connections with potential funders, seeking out training and resources, and learning from feedback, nonprofits can develop strong grant proposals and increase their chances of securing funding.

Another practical example

The organization "Community Health Advocates" (CHA) provides health education and advocacy services to underserved communities in a large urban area. With a small staff of only five people, they struggled with limited capacity and resources to secure grant funding for their programs.

To address this challenge, CHA sought assistance from a local nonprofit resource center that provided grant writing training and technical assistance. The center offered several workshops on grant writing basics, proposal development, and funder research, which the CHA staff attended.

After the training, CHA developed a plan to prioritize funding opportunities that aligned with their organization's mission and programs. They also created a calendar to track grant application deadlines and ensure timely submission.

Despite their efforts, CHA faced several rejections from grant funders due to limited experience and a lack of strong community partnerships. However, they did not let these rejections discourage them. Instead, they used the feedback provided by the funders to improve their proposals and strengthen their relationships with community partners.

To address the issue of limited experience, CHA reached out to other organizations in their field and sought out mentorship and guidance from experienced grant writers. This enabled them to learn best practices and gain insights into successful grant writing strategies.

To address the issue of weak community partnerships, CHA began to collaborate with other nonprofits and community organizations to build strong networks and partnerships. By working together, they were able to leverage each other's strengths and resources, leading to successful grant applications and program implementation.

With the support of the resource center, mentorship from experienced grant writers, and strategic partnerships with community organizations, CHA was able to overcome the challenges of limited staff capacity and lack of experience. They secured several grants and were able to expand their programs, reaching more underserved communities and making a positive impact on the health and wellbeing of the people they serve.

Chapter 10:
Best Practices for Successful Grant Writing

Writing a successful grant proposal can be a daunting task, but there are certain best practices that can help increase your chances of securing funding. In this chapter, we will explore some of these best practices and provide tips for crafting a compelling grant proposal.

1. **Research the funder**: Before you start writing your grant proposal, it's essential to research the funder thoroughly. This will help you understand their mission, values, and priorities and tailor your proposal accordingly. Look for any guidelines or requirements they have for grant proposals, and make sure to follow them precisely.
2. **Clearly state your goals and objectives**: Your grant proposal should clearly state your organization's goals and objectives, the problem you're trying to solve, and the specific outcomes you hope to achieve with the grant funding. Be specific about how you plan to use the funding and how it will help you achieve your goals.
3. **Focus on outcomes**: Funders want to see that their funding will make a difference. Instead of focusing on activities, focus on outcomes. In other words, explain what results you hope to achieve, not just what you plan to do.
4. **Use data to support your proposal**: Using data can help you make a more compelling case for your proposal. Use statistics and other evidence to demonstrate the need for your program, the impact it will have, and the effectiveness of similar programs. Make sure to cite your sources and use data from credible sources.
5. **Tell a compelling story**: While data is essential, it's also important to tell a compelling story about your organization and the people it serves. Use personal stories, anecdotes,

and examples to help funders understand the impact your organization has on individuals and communities.

6. **Make your budget clear and detailed**: Your budget is an essential part of your grant proposal. Make sure to provide a clear and detailed budget that includes all expenses associated with your program. Be realistic and transparent, and make sure your budget aligns with the goals and objectives of your proposal.

7. **Provide a strong evaluation plan:** Funders want to see that you have a plan in place to measure the success of your program. Provide a detailed evaluation plan that includes specific metrics and data collection methods. Make sure to tie your evaluation plan to your goals and objectives and explain how you will use the data to make improvements.

8. **Have a strong project team**: Having a strong project team is essential to the success of your program. Make sure to highlight the qualifications and experience of your team members in your proposal. Show that you have the expertise and capacity to execute the program effectively.

9. **Submit your proposal on time**: Submitting your proposal on time is critical. Make sure to follow all deadlines and submission requirements. Don't wait until the last minute to submit your proposal, as unexpected technical difficulties or other issues can arise.

10. **Follow up with the funder**: After you submit your proposal, make sure to follow up with the funder. Thank them for considering your proposal and provide any additional information they may need. If you receive funding, make sure to keep the funder informed about the progress of your program and provide regular updates and reports.

Developing a Culture of Grant Readiness in your Nonprofit

As a nonprofit organization, grants can be an important source of funding for your programs and projects.

However, successfully securing grants requires more than just writing a strong proposal. It requires a culture of grant readiness within your organization, which involves ongoing planning, relationship building, and capacity building.

Here are some tips for developing a culture of grant readiness within your nonprofit:

1. **Start with a strategic plan:** A strategic plan outlines your nonprofit's goals and objectives, and serves as a roadmap for achieving them. It's important to align your grant-seeking efforts with your organization's overall mission and priorities. By having a clear strategic plan, you can identify which grant opportunities are the best fit for your organization, and focus your efforts on those.

2. **Build relationships with funders**: Establishing relationships with potential funders is critical to your success in securing grants. Reach out to funders, attend their events and conferences, and make an effort to understand their priorities and funding criteria. By building relationships with funders, you can learn about grant opportunities before they are publicly announced, and increase your chances of being awarded a grant.

3. **Develop your grant-seeking team**: Developing a team of individuals with the right skills and experience is critical to successful grant writing. Identify team members with experience in grant writing, budgeting, and program planning. Assign roles and responsibilities to team members, and ensure that everyone is working together towards a common goal.

4. **Train your team**: Training is key to building a culture of grant readiness. Provide your team with ongoing professional development opportunities that will help them build their skills in grant writing, budgeting, and program planning. This will help them to be better equipped to successfully secure grant funding for your organization.

5. **Prepare in advance**: Developing a grant proposal requires a lot of time and effort, so it's important to start early and prepare in advance. Create a grant calendar that outlines all of the upcoming grant opportunities that your organization will be applying for. This will help you stay on top of deadlines and ensure that you have enough time to develop a high-quality proposal.

6. **Review and evaluate**: Once you have secured grant funding, it's important to review and evaluate your grant activities regularly. This will help you to track progress towards your goals, identify any challenges, and make adjustments as needed. By tracking and evaluating your grant activities, you can also gather data that can be used in future grant applications.

Collaborating Effectively with Partners and Stakeholders

Collaborating with partners and stakeholders is an essential component of successful grant writing. Partnerships and collaborations can bring in additional expertise, resources, and support for your nonprofit's projects. It also allows for greater reach and impact of your organization's work. Effective collaboration with partners and stakeholders requires clear communication, mutual trust and respect, and a shared commitment to achieving the project's goals. In this article, we will explore some best practices for collaborating effectively with partners and stakeholders in grant writing.

1. Identify Your Partners and Stakeholders

Before beginning any collaboration, it's important to identify potential partners and stakeholders. These can be other nonprofits, community organizations, government agencies, and individuals who share your organization's goals and values. Consider the expertise and resources they can bring to the table and how they can complement your organization's strengths.

2. Develop a Shared Vision

Once you have identified potential partners and stakeholders, it's essential to develop a shared vision for the project. This shared vision should be based on your common goals and values. This shared vision will ensure that everyone is working towards the same objectives, and it provides clarity and direction for the project.

3. Establish Clear Roles and Responsibilities

Establishing clear roles and responsibilities for each partner is key to effective collaboration. This helps to ensure that everyone knows what is expected of them, and it helps to avoid misunderstandings and conflicts. Each partner should have a clearly defined role and responsibility that reflects their strengths and expertise.

4. Communicate Effectively

Clear and open communication is essential to the success of any collaboration. It's important to establish clear communication channels and protocols that ensure everyone is kept informed and up-to-date. Effective communication includes listening actively, providing feedback, and being responsive to others' needs.

5. Build Trust and Respect

Building trust and respect is key to effective collaboration. Trust and respect are built through open and honest communication, a shared commitment to the project, and a willingness to work through challenges together. Building trust takes time and requires consistent effort from all parties.

6. Establish Metrics for Success

Establishing metrics for success is essential to ensure that the project is on track and achieving its goals. These metrics can be developed collaboratively with partners and stakeholders and should be measurable, achievable, and relevant to the project's objectives.

7. Evaluate and Learn

Effective collaboration requires continuous evaluation and learning. Regular evaluation of the collaboration and the project helps to identify areas of success and areas for improvement. Learning from the successes and failures of the collaboration can help to improve future collaborations.

In conclusion, collaborating effectively with partners and stakeholders is essential for successful grant writing. It requires clear communication, mutual trust and respect, a shared commitment to the project, and a willingness to work through challenges together. By following these best practices, your nonprofit can develop strong partnerships and collaborations that can bring greater impact and reach to your projects.

Building Long-Term Relationships with Funders,

Building long-term relationships with funders is a critical component of successful grant writing for nonprofits. Establishing these relationships can help organizations secure funding for future projects, build credibility within their field, and potentially even unlock new opportunities for growth and expansion. In this article, we'll explore some best practices for building and maintaining strong relationships with funders.

1. **Communicate effectively and regularly**: One of the most important aspects of building strong relationships with funders is effective communication. This means more than simply submitting polished grant proposals on time, but also communicating regularly throughout the grant cycle and beyond. Keeping funders updated on project progress, challenges, and successes can demonstrate a high level of transparency and accountability that can help build trust over time. Consider scheduling regular check-ins or providing progress reports, so funders stay informed about how their investment is making an impact.

2. **Prioritize transparency and accountability**: When it comes to working with funders, transparency and accountability are key. Be upfront about your organization's capabilities and limitations from the outset, and communicate clearly about your goals and how the grant funds will be used. This can help establish a foundation of trust that can last beyond the life of a single grant. Additionally, make sure to document and report on project outcomes in a clear and timely manner, so that funders can see the tangible results of their investment.

3. **Show gratitude and appreciation**: A simple but often overlooked practice for building strong relationships with funders is expressing gratitude and appreciation for their support. A thank-you note or phone call can go a long way in demonstrating that their investment is valued and will be used thoughtfully. Additionally, consider inviting funders to project events or offering other forms of recognition, such as including them in your organization's annual report

or sharing their logo on your website. These small gestures can help deepen relationships and build goodwill over time.

4. Seek **feedback and incorporate it into future proposals:** When grant proposals are rejected, it can be tempting to move on and focus on the next opportunity. However, this approach misses a valuable opportunity to learn and grow. Instead, consider reaching out to funders for feedback on your proposal and using that feedback to refine your approach for future applications. This demonstrates a commitment to improvement and shows funders that you are receptive to their suggestions.

5. **Be flexible and open to collaboration**: Fundraising is often a collaborative effort, and the ability to be flexible and open to collaboration can help build stronger relationships with funders. This means being open to feedback, exploring alternative funding sources or partnership opportunities, and adapting to new project requirements as they arise. By demonstrating that your organization is adaptable and responsive, you may be better positioned to secure additional funding and build lasting relationships with funders.

CASE STUDY

Nonprofits rely heavily on grant funding to support their missions, programs, and services. To secure this funding, nonprofits must be strategic in their approach to grant writing, collaboration with partners and stakeholders, and building relationships with funders. In this practical example, we will explore successful strategies used by top-performing nonprofits, which can serve as a blueprint for any nonprofit seeking to secure grant funding and build sustainable relationships with funders.

Building Strong Partnerships with Other Organizations

Collaboration with other organizations can be a powerful strategy for achieving shared goals, accessing new resources, and expanding the reach of your programs and services. Successful nonprofits prioritize building strong partnerships and seek out organizations that share similar missions and values.

For example, one nonprofit, a community-based organization focused on providing job training and education for underserved populations, partnered with a local workforce development agency to expand its reach and resources. By collaborating with the workforce development agency, the nonprofit was able to offer additional job training programs and resources, reach new populations, and leverage the agency's expertise and connections to secure additional funding.

To successfully collaborate with partners, nonprofits should focus on developing relationships built on trust and mutual respect, clear communication, and shared goals. This involves investing time and resources in building relationships with potential partners, understanding their needs and goals, and identifying areas of shared interest and potential collaboration.

Developing a Culture of Grant Readiness

To secure grant funding, nonprofits must be prepared to respond to opportunities as they arise. This requires a culture of grant readiness, which involves having a deep understanding of your organization's programs and services, an up-to-date understanding of the grant landscape, and a commitment to continuous improvement and learning.

One way to build a culture of grant readiness is to establish a cross-functional grant team responsible for researching, writing, and managing grants. The team should be comprised of individuals with diverse skills and expertise, including program staff, finance and accounting, and communication and marketing. By bringing together a team with a range of skills and expertise, nonprofits can ensure that their grant proposals are well-rounded and address all aspects of the program or service being proposed.

Nonprofits can also invest in professional development for their staff to build their knowledge and skills in grant writing and management. This includes attending conferences and workshops, participating in webinars and online courses, and seeking out mentorship and coaching opportunities.

Prioritizing Long-Term Relationships with Funders

Building long-term relationships with funders is essential for securing ongoing support for your programs and services. Successful nonprofits prioritize building strong relationships with funders and view grant funding as a partnership, not just a transaction.

One way to build long-term relationships with funders is to prioritize clear and regular communication. This includes providing regular updates on program and service outcomes, inviting funders to visit your organization and see your work in action, and soliciting feedback and input from funders on how to improve your programs and services.

Another key strategy for building long-term relationships with funders is to focus on stewardship and impact. Nonprofits should prioritize effective grant management *and reporting, providing funders with accurate and timely financial and programmatic reports, and showcasing the impact of their programs and services.*

By building long-term relationships with funders, nonprofits can position themselves as reliable and trusted partners, increasing the likelihood of ongoing funding and support for their mission and programs.

Chapter 11:
Conclusion: Mastering Grant Writing for Lasting Impact

Grant writing is a critical process for nonprofit organizations seeking funding to make an impact in their communities. Writing a successful grant proposal can be a challenging task that requires careful planning, attention to detail, and collaboration with partners and stakeholders.

In this final chapter, we will summarize some of the key takeaways from this guide and provide some concluding thoughts on how nonprofits can master the grant writing process for lasting impact.

The grant writing process involves several key steps, including identifying potential funding opportunities, researching the funder's priorities and requirements, developing a compelling proposal, and managing the grant funds effectively. While each step presents unique challenges, there are some best practices that can help nonprofits overcome these challenges and achieve success.

One of the most important strategies for successful grant writing is to develop a culture of grant readiness within the organization. This involves ensuring that all staff members are aware of the organization's mission and goals and understand how grant funding can help achieve these goals. It also involves building relationships with potential funders and partners, developing strong project ideas, and maintaining accurate records of grant activity.

Another critical component of successful grant writing is collaboration with partners and stakeholders. By working with other organizations, nonprofits can leverage their resources and expertise to develop innovative and impactful projects that are more likely to receive funding. This requires effective communication and coordination between partners, as well as a willingness to share credit and recognize the contributions of each partner.

Finally, building long-term relationships with funders is essential for lasting impact. This involves maintaining open lines of communication with funders, providing regular updates on grant activity, and demonstrating the impact of grant funds through clear and accurate reporting. By building trust and demonstrating a commitment to the funder's priorities and goals, nonprofits can increase their chances of receiving future funding and achieving lasting impact.

As we come to the end of this guide, it is important to remember that successful grant writing is about more than just securing funding. It is about developing innovative projects that address critical needs in the community, building strong partnerships, and achieving lasting impact. While the process can be challenging, it is also rewarding, and can help nonprofit organizations achieve their goals and make a positive difference in the world.

By following the best practices outlined in this guide, nonprofit organizations can increase their chances of securing funding and achieving lasting impact. However, it is important to remember that each funder is unique and may have different requirements and priorities. It is essential to do the research and tailor each proposal to the specific needs and goals of the funder.

It is also important to recognize that grant writing is not a one-time event, but an ongoing process. Even after securing funding, nonprofits must continue to manage the grant funds effectively, maintain open lines of communication with the funder, and report on the impact of the grant. By demonstrating a commitment to transparency and accountability, nonprofits can build trust with funders and increase their chances of securing future funding.

In conclusion, successful grant writing requires careful planning, collaboration with partners and stakeholders, and a commitment to best practices. By developing a culture of grant readiness, collaborating effectively, and building long-term relationships with funders, nonprofits can maximize their impact and achieve lasting success. We hope this guide has provided useful insights and strategies for nonprofit organizations seeking to master the grant writing process for lasting impact.

Celebrating your successes and learning from failures
Grant writing can be a challenging but rewarding process, and it's important to celebrate your successes and learn from your failures. Celebrating your successes can help you maintain momentum and motivate you to continue pursuing grant opportunities. Learning from your failures can help you identify areas for improvement and develop stronger proposals in the future.

When you receive a grant award, take time to celebrate your accomplishment. Share the news with your team, stakeholders, and funders, and express your gratitude for their support. Celebrate the impact that the grant will have on your organization and the community you serve.

It's also important to track your progress and measure the impact of your grant-funded project. Regularly assess your progress towards your goals, and adjust your strategies if necessary. Collect data and feedback from program participants, and use that information to improve your services and programs.

However, not all grant applications will be successful, and it's important to learn from your failures. If your proposal is rejected, try to obtain feedback from the funder to understand why it was not funded. This feedback can be valuable in helping you identify areas for improvement and refine your future grant proposals.

Don't take rejection as a reflection of your organization's worth or value. It's important to remember that grant writing is a highly competitive process, and funders receive many more proposals than they can fund. Even highly qualified organizations can be turned down due to factors such as limited funding or a highly competitive pool of applicants.

Instead, use the feedback to identify areas for improvement and strengthen your proposals for the future. Consider revising your proposal based on the feedback received, or seeking advice from a grant writing consultant or mentor to help you refine your approach.

Remember that grant writing is a process, and success often comes through persistence and resilience. Celebrate your successes, learn from your failures, and continue to refine your approach to grant writing. With dedication and effort, you can make a lasting impact on your organization and the communities you serve.

Sustaining a Strong Grants Program over Time
Grants can be a major source of funding for nonprofit organizations, but they can also be time-consuming and challenging to secure. Once a nonprofit has successfully secured a grant, it's important to sustain a strong grant

program over time. This can help ensure continued funding and support for the organization's mission and programs.

Here are some key strategies for sustaining a strong grants program:

1. **Develop a grants management plan**

   A grants management plan can help ensure that your organization is using grant funds effectively and efficiently. This plan should outline the roles and responsibilities of staff members involved in grant management, as well as timelines for reporting and other requirements. It should also include policies and procedures for managing grant funds, such as financial reporting and compliance with funder requirements.

2. **Build relationships with funders**

   Building relationships with funders can help ensure that your organization is top of mind when new grant opportunities arise. Stay in touch with funders by providing regular updates on your organization's progress and impact, and invite them to visit your programs and events. When applying for new grants, be sure to tailor your proposal to the funder's specific interests and requirements.

3. **Track and report on outcomes**

   Funders want to see evidence of the impact their grant is having. Be sure to track and report on outcomes related to the grant, such as the number of people served, improvements in program quality, or changes in policy. Use data and stories to illustrate the impact of the grant and make a compelling case for continued funding.

4. Invest in professional development

Professional development can help staff members build the skills and knowledge needed to secure and manage grants effectively. Consider providing training in grant writing, financial management, and other key areas. Encourage staff members to attend conferences and workshops, and offer opportunities for networking and collaboration with other nonprofit professionals.

5. Engage volunteers

Volunteers can be a valuable resource for sustaining a strong grants program. Consider recruiting volunteers with expertise in grant writing, fundraising, or other related areas. Engage volunteers in reviewing grant proposals, researching new grant opportunities, or managing the grants management plan.

6. Diversify funding sources

While grants can be a valuable source of funding, it's important to diversify your organization's funding sources to reduce reliance on any one funding stream. Consider other fundraising strategies such as individual giving, major gifts, or corporate sponsorships. Diversifying funding sources can help ensure the long-term sustainability of your organization's programs and mission.

7. Stay up-to-date on best practices

The world of grant writing and grant management is constantly evolving. Staying up-to-date on best practices can help your organization stay competitive and effective. Read grant-related publications and blogs, attend conferences and workshops, and participate in online forums and discussions.

By following these strategies, your organization can sustain a strong grants program over time, leading to continued funding and support for your important work.

Making a Lasting Impact through Effective Grant Writing and Management,

Grants are an essential tool for nonprofits seeking to create lasting change in their communities. However, securing funding through grants is just the beginning of a long journey to create a lasting impact. Effective grant writing and management are necessary to turn grant funding into real-world results that make a difference in the lives of people and communities.

To make a lasting impact through effective grant writing and management, nonprofits must focus on a few critical areas.

The first area is program design. The most effective grant programs are those that are well-designed and focused on specific outcomes. Nonprofits must ensure that their programs are designed to achieve measurable outcomes that align with their mission and values. By developing clear program objectives, identifying target populations, and articulating strategies for achieving program goals, nonprofits can design programs that are more likely to achieve long-lasting impact.

The second area is project management. Effective project management is essential for turning grant funding into real-world results. Nonprofits must establish clear timelines, milestones, and budgets to ensure that programs are implemented effectively and efficiently. They must also establish monitoring and evaluation processes to track progress and make adjustments as needed.

The third area is building relationships with funders and other stakeholders. Nonprofits must develop strong relationships with funders and stakeholders to ensure that their programs are well-supported and sustainable over the long term. This includes establishing effective communication channels, providing regular updates and progress reports, and engaging with funders and **stakeholders to understand their needs and priorities.**

The fourth area is fostering a culture of learning and continuous improvement. Nonprofits must be committed to learning from their experiences, both successes and failures, to continuously improve their grant programs. This includes establishing systems for evaluating program effectiveness, collecting feedback from stakeholders, and making necessary adjustments to improve program **outcomes.**

The fifth and final area is leveraging technology and data to improve program outcomes. Nonprofits must leverage technology and data to improve program outcomes and support evidence-based decision-making. By using data to monitor and evaluate program outcomes, nonprofits can identify areas for improvement and make data-driven decisions to improve program effectiveness.

In conclusion, making a lasting impact through effective grant writing and management requires a multifaceted approach that focuses on program design, project management, building relationships with funders and stakeholders, fostering a culture of learning and continuous improvement, and leveraging technology and data. By prioritizing these areas, nonprofits can turn grant funding into real-world results that create lasting change in their communities.

TAKEAWAYS

As we come to the end of this book, we hope that you have gained valuable insights into the world of grant writing and management. You have learned about the key components of a successful grant proposal, how to find and approach potential funders, strategies for building strong relationships with stakeholders, and best practices for managing grants and reporting to funders. Now, let's summarize some key takeaways and provide additional resources for nonprofits looking to improve their grant writing skills.

Key Takeaways:

1. Develop a culture of grant readiness: It's important to develop a culture of grant readiness within your organization. This means having a clear understanding of your mission and goals, strong communication and collaboration skills, and a willingness to continuously learn and improve your grant writing and management skills.
2. Build strong partnerships: Strong partnerships with other organizations can help you achieve your goals and make a lasting impact. Look for organizations that share your values and goals, and explore ways to work together to achieve mutual success.
3. Prioritize long-term relationships with funders: It's important to build strong relationships with funders and maintain those relationships over time. This means staying in touch, providing regular updates on your progress, and being responsive to feedback.

4. Be proactive and strategic: Don't wait for grant opportunities to come to you. Be proactive in seeking out potential funders and strategic in your approach to grant writing and management.
5. Celebrate your successes and learn from failures: Celebrate your successes, no matter how small they may seem. Take the time to reflect on what went well and what could be improved, and use that knowledge to make informed decisions and continuously improve.

Inspiring stories:

One inspiring example of a nonprofit that has made a lasting impact through effective grant writing and management is Charity: Water. This organization has raised over $500 million to provide clean and safe drinking water to people in need around the world. Charity: Water has been able to achieve this through a combination of strong partnerships, a focus on transparency and accountability, and a commitment to continuous learning and improvement.

If you're looking to improve your grant writing and management skills, there are many resources available to help you. Here are a few that we recommend:

1. The Foundation Center: The Foundation Center is a great resource for nonprofits looking to find potential funders, learn about the grant writing process, and access a variety of other resources and tools.
2. GrantStation: GrantStation is another resource that provides information on funding opportunities, grant writing tips, and more.
3. The Chronicle of Philanthropy: The Chronicle of Philanthropy is a leading source of news and information

for the nonprofit sector, and offers a variety of resources on grant writing and management.

4. Nonprofit Ready: Nonprofit Ready offers a wide range of free online courses on grant writing and management, as well as other important skills for nonprofit professionals.

In conclusion, effective grant writing and management can help nonprofits achieve their goals and make a lasting impact in their communities. By developing a culture of grant readiness, building strong partnerships, prioritizing long-term relationships with funders, being proactive and strategic, and celebrating your successes and learning from failures, you can create a strong and sustainable grants program. Remember, there are many resources available to help you improve your grant writing and management skills, so don't be afraid to seek them out and take advantage of them

Another inspiring stories

One example is the National Park Foundation, which works to protect and preserve America's national parks for future generations. The Foundation has been able to secure millions of dollars in grant funding to support their work, including a recent $5 million grant from the Lilly Endowment.

To successfully secure grant funding, the National Park Foundation has prioritized building strong relationships with funders and partners. They have worked to establish themselves as a trusted and reliable organization in the eyes of potential funders, and have been able to leverage these relationships to secure significant grant funding.

In addition to building strong partnerships, the National Park Foundation has also made a concerted effort to develop a culture of grant readiness within their organization. They have invested in staff training and development, and have worked to ensure that all team members are familiar with the grant writing process and requirements.

Finally, the National Park Foundation has prioritized long-term relationships with funders, recognizing that building strong partnerships takes time and effort. By maintaining regular communication with funders and keeping them up-to-date on their progress and impact, the National Park Foundation has been able to secure repeat funding and establish themselves as a reliable and effective organization.

Through their focus on building partnerships, developing a culture of grant readiness, and prioritizing long-term relationships, the National Park Foundation has been able to make a lasting impact on the conservation of America's national parks. Their success serves as an inspiration to other nonprofits looking to improve their grant writing and management skills.

- **The Fistula Foundation** - The Fistula Foundation is a nonprofit organization that works to prevent and treat obstetric fistula, a devastating childbirth injury that affects millions of women in developing countries. Through effective grant writing and management, the organization has been able to provide life-changing surgery and medical care to thousands of women, as well as to support community outreach and education programs to prevent fistula from occurring in the first place. The

Fistula Foundation has built strong relationships with funders and donors, and has been recognized for its transparency and accountability in the use of grant funds.

- **Team Rubicon** - Team Rubicon is a disaster response organization that mobilizes veterans and civilians to provide emergency relief in the aftermath of natural disasters and other crises. Through its grant writing and management efforts, the organization has been able to secure funding from a wide range of sources, including government agencies, private foundations, and corporate partners. Team Rubicon has also developed strong partnerships with other nonprofits and community organizations, which has enabled it to leverage resources and expertise to maximize its impact.

- **The Trevor Project** - The Trevor Project is a national organization that provides crisis intervention and suicide prevention services to LGBTQ+ youth. Through its grant writing and management efforts, the organization has been able to expand its reach and impact, providing support to millions of young people in crisis. The Trevor Project has also been successful in building long-term relationships with funders, including major corporations and foundations, which has allowed it to sustain and grow its programs over time.

These organizations demonstrate the power of effective grant writing and management to make a lasting impact in the world. By building strong relationships with funders and partners, developing a culture of grant readiness, and prioritizing long-term sustainability, nonprofits can achieve their goals and make a meaningful difference in the lives of those they serve.

CONTACT
EMAIL: grantwritingacademy@gmail.com
Website: grantwritingacad.org

About The Book

As a nonprofit, securing funding is essential to achieving your mission and creating lasting impact in your community. But the grant writing process can be daunting, with many obstacles to overcome and skills to master. That's where "Mastering Grant Writing: A Comprehensive Guide for Nonprofits" comes in.

This comprehensive guide provides a step-by-step approach to the grant writing process, from identifying potential funders and crafting a compelling proposal to effectively managing grant funds and building long-term relationships with funders. Through practical tips, real-world examples, and expert advice, this book will equip you with the skills and knowledge needed to succeed in securing and managing grant funding.

You will learn how to develop a culture of grant readiness, collaborate effectively with partners and stakeholders, and overcome common grant writing challenges. You will also discover how to celebrate your successes and learn from failures, creating a sustainable and successful grants program over time.

In addition to the comprehensive guide, "Mastering Grant Writing" includes inspiring stories of nonprofits that have successfully secured and managed grant funding, highlighting the best practices and strategies they used to achieve lasting impact in their communities.

Whether you are new to grant writing or looking to enhance your skills and knowledge, "Mastering Grant Writing: A Comprehensive Guide for Nonprofits" is an essential resource for any nonprofit looking to make a difference. With the support of your team, including your spouse and children, you can take the necessary steps to secure the funding needed to create real change in the world.

www.ingramcontent.com/pod-product-compliance
Lightning Source LLC
Chambersburg PA
CBHW071136220526
45467CB00015B/1177